MATTHEW EXPLAINED

MATTHEW EXPLAINED

Understanding the Book and Its Message for Today

Samuel Whitaker

Part of the Bible for Modern Life Series

Ascent Press

Published by
Ascent Press

ISBN: 978-1-972885-01-7

Printed in the United States of America

First Edition 2026

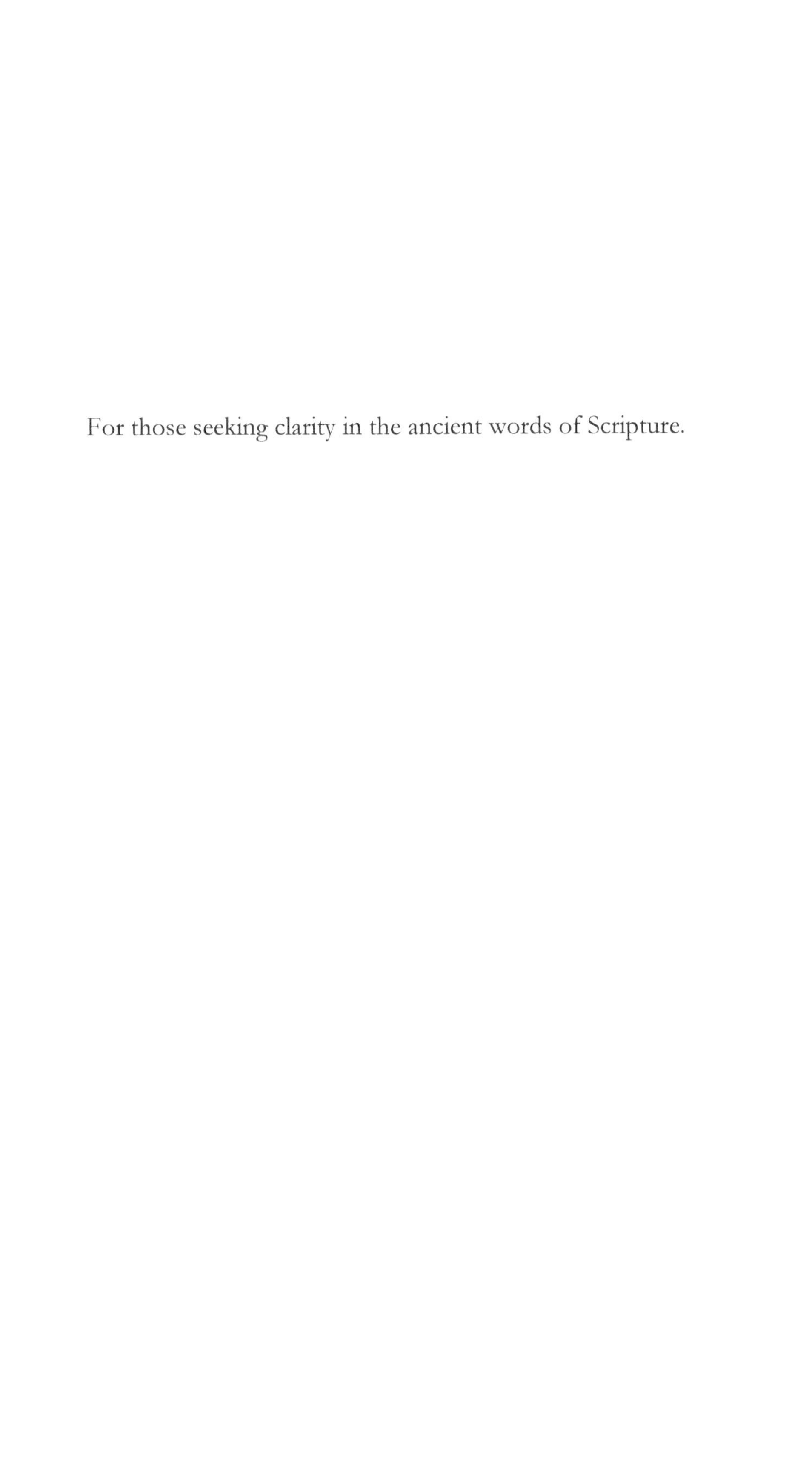

For those seeking clarity in the ancient words of Scripture.

CONTENTS

Disclaimer

This book provides an interpretive overview of the biblical text using historical scholarship and modern analysis tools. It is intended to help readers understand the themes, context, and message of the biblical narrative and is not intended to replace personal study of Scripture

Introduction

Why Matthew Still Matters

Of the four Gospels, Matthew is the one most thoroughly rooted in the world of the Hebrew Bible. Its author wrote not only to tell the story of Jesus but to demonstrate something — to show, through careful arrangement of narrative and teaching, that the figure at the center of this account was the fulfillment of everything Israel had been given to hope for. The book opens with a genealogy that traces its subject back through David to Abraham, the founding father of the covenant people. It ends with a command that reaches beyond the boundaries of Israel to every nation on earth. In between, it unfolds the most comprehensive portrait of Jesus' teaching found anywhere in the New Testament.

That range — from the deep roots of Jewish covenant history to the global scope of a final commission — gives Matthew its distinctive character. It is simultaneously the most Jewish of the Gospels and the most explicitly universal. It preserves more of Jesus' extended teaching than any other account, organizing that teaching into five major discourses that scholars have long recognized as a deliberate structural feature. It situates the story of Jesus within a carefully constructed narrative framework that moves from announcement and preparation through ministry, conflict, and death to resurrection and renewed mission.

For modern readers, Matthew can feel initially familiar — many of its most beloved passages appear here for the first time or in their fullest form. The Beatitudes, the Lord's Prayer, the Sermon on the Mount, the Great Commission — these are not incidental features of Matthew but central expressions of its theological vision. Yet the familiarity of individual passages can obscure the depth of the whole. Matthew is not a collection of memorable sayings. It is a carefully constructed argument about who Jesus is, what his coming means, and what life in response to that coming requires. Readers who approach it only through isolated verses tend to miss the sustained argument that gives those verses their full weight and their proper context.

Understanding Matthew well requires some orientation — to the historical world that produced it, to the literary strategies that shape it, to the theological claims that run through it from beginning to end. This book aims to provide that orientation. Rather than examining every verse or passage in detail, it focuses on the larger patterns: the historical setting that shaped Matthew's perspective, the themes that recur throughout the narrative, the structure that organizes the whole, and the ways Matthew's portrait of Jesus continues to address the deepest questions of human existence.

Matthew is not a document for specialists. It was written for communities of faith trying to understand who they were in light of what had happened in Jesus, and it continues to address communities in the same position. The goal of this book is to help modern readers approach it with the understanding it deserves — and to discover in it what generations of readers before them have found: a portrait of Jesus that is richer, deeper, and more demanding than any single reading can exhaust.

Chapter 1

The Human Question

*"Come to me, all you who are weary and burdened, and I will give
you rest. Take my yoke upon you and learn from me, for I am
gentle and humble in heart, and you will find rest for your souls."*
— Matthew 11:28–29 (NIV)

The Universal Search for Meaning

Every generation inherits the same set of questions. They arrive dressed in different vocabularies and weighted with different anxieties, but their core structure is remarkably consistent: What makes a life worth living? Where does the authority that commands my loyalty come from? What am I supposed to do with guilt, with failure, with the gap between who I am and who I know I should be? These are not questions that education eliminates or prosperity dissolves. They persist at the center of human experience regardless of the century or culture in which they arise.

The Gospel of Matthew takes these questions seriously. It does not sidestep them or dissolve them into comfortable reassurances. Instead, it presents a figure — Jesus of Nazareth — as the one in whom these questions find their most searching answer. Not through abstract philosophical argument, but through narrative: through the account of what this person said and did, how he responded to the suffering and confusion of ordinary human beings, what his presence made possible, and what his death and resurrection finally meant.

Understanding why Matthew was written requires recognizing the specific human context it addresses. The earliest communities that read this Gospel were not academic inquirers sitting comfortably at a distance from its claims. They were people navigating the collapse of familiar structures, the disruption of inherited communities, and the pressure of having committed themselves to a set of convictions that set them apart from the world around them. They needed clarity about who Jesus was, why his story mattered, and what it meant for their own daily lives to follow him.

What makes Matthew's approach to these questions distinctive is the way it refuses to separate them from one another. The question of meaning and the question of authority and the question of genuine fulfillment are, in Matthew's telling, the same question approached from different angles. They all converge on the person of Jesus — not as one possible answer among several, but as the answer that reshapes every dimension of the question. Matthew does not offer a philosophy of life with Jesus as one of its illustrations. It offers a portrait of a person and insists that encountering this person adequately is itself the resolution of the questions that human experience generates most persistently.

This is a demanding claim, and Matthew is not unaware of the resistance it will meet. The Gospel is written for people who already know something of Jesus, who have already made some form of commitment in response to what they know, and who are now trying to understand more deeply what that commitment means and what it requires. It is a document of formation as much as of information — designed not merely to convey accurate theology about Jesus but to produce people whose lives have been genuinely shaped by encounter with him. The questions it addresses are not resolved by reading the Gospel once with careful attention. They are the questions that the Gospel keeps pressing, through every narrative and every discourse, toward the reader who is willing to keep being pressed.

The Exhaustion of Human Effort

One of the most striking features of the human condition that Matthew's Gospel addresses is a particular kind of exhaustion — the weariness that comes not from laziness but from effort that has not found its proper rest. The people Jesus encounters throughout Matthew are not, for the most part, passive or indifferent. They are burdened. The crowds that follow him through the countryside are described with notable compassion: harassed and helpless, like sheep without a shepherd. The scribes and Pharisees are not passive either — they are intensely active, working hard to maintain the frameworks of meaning and obligation that define their world. Yet Matthew's portrait suggests that effort alone, even sincere and serious effort, is not sufficient to provide the rest that human beings fundamentally need.

This is not a counsel of passivity. Jesus does not call people to stop engaging with their lives or to abandon the responsibilities they carry. He calls them to take on a different yoke — his own — and to discover in the relationship it creates a quality of engagement with life that labor alone cannot produce. The invitation is not to less but to different: a life shaped by relationship with him rather than by the unaided effort to meet every demand through personal willpower and compliance.

For modern readers, this dynamic is recognizable even outside explicitly religious contexts. There is a familiar quality to the experience of working hard, meeting obligations, performing what is expected, and still feeling that something essential is missing — that the effort does not finally satisfy the deeper need it was supposed to address. Matthew's opening portrait of human need suggests that this experience is not simply the result of insufficient effort. It points toward a different kind of problem, one that requires a different kind of solution.

The yoke metaphor that appears in Matthew's invitation deserves particular attention because it does considerable theological work in a small space. In first-century Jewish usage, a yoke was commonly a metaphor for the obligations of Torah — the whole system of commands and their interpretation that shaped the daily life of the covenant community. To take on the yoke of Torah was to accept its authority and to submit to its disciplines. When Jesus offers his own yoke as an alternative, he is not simply offering a lighter set of requirements. He is presenting himself as the one whose relationship with those who follow him creates the conditions in which the deeper purposes of the law — the formation of people genuinely oriented toward God and toward one another — can actually be accomplished.

This means that the exhaustion Matthew's Gospel addresses is not merely physical or psychological. It is the exhaustion of a form of religious life that has become organized around performance rather than relationship, around compliance rather than transformation, around the careful management of obligations rather than the reorientation of the whole self around the one who gives those obligations their meaning. The rest that Jesus offers is not the rest of having fewer things to do. It is the rest of doing everything from within a relationship that provides what effort alone cannot: a genuinely different orientation of the interior life from which everything outward flows.

The crowds who follow Jesus through the Galilean countryside represent something broader than the specific population of first-century Palestine. They represent the human condition in its universally recognizable form: people who are doing their best within the frameworks available to them and discovering that their best is not quite enough, that the frameworks themselves are not quite equal to the weight they are being asked to bear. Matthew presents Jesus not as a critic of these people's effort but as the one who recognizes it with compassion and who offers something the effort cannot produce for itself. This is the pastoral heart of the Gospel from its earliest chapters

— not condemnation of the struggling but the offer of a different kind of help than the struggling have been able to find.

The Question of Authority

Alongside the question of human exhaustion, Matthew's Gospel raises with unusual directness the question of authority. The crowds who hear Jesus teach are described as astonished — not because his content is unfamiliar but because of the way he speaks. He teaches as one who has authority, not as their scribes teach. This distinction is not primarily about confidence or rhetorical skill. It is about the source of what is being said.

The scribal tradition that shaped first-century Jewish religious life operated by citation and precedent. Authority was derived from the chain of interpretation that connected present practice to the accumulated wisdom of the tradition. Jesus does not operate within that framework. He cites the tradition — you have heard that it was said — and then supersedes it: but I say to you. This is not a claim to superior scholarship. It is a claim to a different kind of standing entirely.

Matthew's Gospel is deeply interested in the question of where genuine authority comes from. It is a question that arises at the beginning of the narrative and runs through it to the end, where the risen Jesus makes his most explicit claim: all authority in heaven and on earth has been given to me. Everything in between — the teachings, the healings, the controversies, the death and resurrection — is in some sense the content that gives that claim its meaning. Matthew is asking its readers to consider not just what Jesus taught but who Jesus is, because the answer to the second question determines everything about how the first is to be received.

The question of authority is not simply a theological abstraction. It is one of the most practically pressing questions of any era, including the present one. Every person lives under some authority — some account of what is ultimately real, some vision of what genuinely matters, some framework within which choices are made, and lives are organized. The question is never whether authority will shape a life but which authority, and whether that authority is adequate to the weight it is being asked to carry. Matthew's Gospel presses this question with unusual honesty by presenting a figure whose authority is not derived, not borrowed, and not provisional. His authority is his own, which is why the crowds recognize it as different in kind from anything they have encountered before.

The pattern of citation and supersession in the Sermon on the Mount — you have heard that it was said, but I say to you — is sometimes misread as a critique of the Jewish legal tradition, as if Jesus were replacing an inadequate system with a superior one. But Matthew's presentation is more careful than that. Jesus is not opposing the tradition; he is fulfilling it, revealing the interior logic it was always moving toward but had not yet reached in the forms through which it was typically expressed. The authority he exercises is not the authority to dismantle but to complete — to bring the tradition to the fullness of meaning it was designed to carry from the beginning. This is a different kind of authority claim than any the scribal tradition could accommodate, which is precisely why the astonishment of the crowds is the appropriate response.

The Longing for Something New

Matthew's Gospel also addresses a specifically Jewish longing — the expectation, shaped by centuries of prophetic promise, that God would act decisively to fulfill what had been spoken over Israel. This was not a longing for private spiritual experience. It was a corporate hope for the restoration of God's people, the arrival of the messianic age, and the renewal of creation. The prophetic tradition had kept this hope alive through periods of conquest, exile, and occupation, and it continued to animate Jewish life in the first century.

Matthew presents Jesus as the one in whom this corporate longing finds its unexpected fulfillment. The genealogy that opens the book situates Jesus within the line of Abraham and David — the two figures around whom Israel's covenant hope was concentrated. The formula quotations that appear throughout the narrative — this happened to fulfill what was spoken by the prophet — are not merely ornamental. They are Matthew's sustained argument that the story of Jesus is not a departure from the story of Israel but its culmination.

This does not mean that Matthew presents a neat or untroubled fulfillment. The arrival of the one long promised is met with hostility as well as welcome, with rejection by religious authorities even as it draws the sick, the outcast, and the marginalized. The fulfillment of Israel's hope comes in a form that many within Israel do not recognize. Matthew holds this tension without resolving it into easy categories, and in doing so, it addresses a question that extends far beyond first-century Judaism: why does genuine fulfillment so often come in forms that the people who most longed for it are least prepared to receive?

The longing for something genuinely new — for a different order of things than what the present moment offers — is not exclusive to first-century Judaism. It is a feature of human experience across every cultural context and every historical period. What Matthew's engagement with Jewish messianic expectation offers to readers from every background is a window into the dynamics of hope and its fulfillment that remain consistent regardless of the specific form the hope takes. The pattern it reveals is this: genuine fulfillment tends to arrive in a form that cannot be fully recognized by the categories that generated the longing, because those categories were themselves shaped by the limitations of the unfulfilled situation. The arrival of what was hoped for inevitably exceeds and in some measure reshapes the hope itself.

Matthew is not naive about the difficulty this creates. The Gospel does not pretend that the resistance to Jesus among those who held Israel's hope most seriously was irrational or simply willful. It acknowledges the genuine interpretive challenge: how do you recognize the fulfillment of a promise when the fulfillment arrives in a form your reading of the promise did not lead you to expect? This is the question that Matthew itself is designed to help its readers answer, not by resolving the tension too quickly but by sitting with it long enough to allow the portrait of Jesus to do its work — to allow the one who fulfills to define the terms of fulfillment rather than being evaluated by terms he transcends.

The Shape of What Follows

The three questions that Chapter 1 has identified — the question of meaning and rest, the question of genuine authority, and the question of longing and fulfillment — are not three separate concerns that Matthew addresses in three different places. They are three dimensions of a single underlying question that the Gospel engages from every angle throughout its twenty-eight chapters. The chapters that follow will examine the historical world that shaped Matthew's perspective, the literary structure that organizes its argument, the major themes that recur throughout its narrative, the ways it has been misread, and the specific ways it continues to speak to the experience of modern readers.

But all of that examination serves the single purpose of preparing readers to encounter Matthew itself — to read it as a whole rather than in fragments, to allow its argument to develop rather than extracting individual passages from their context, and to bring to it the kind of honest engagement that any serious document deserves. Matthew's portrait of Jesus is not an easy one to receive. It makes demands as well as offers. It challenges as well as comforts. It presses toward a response rather than permitting comfortable distance. Understanding it more fully changes not only how it is read but how it is lived — and that, finally, is the purpose for which it was written.

Chapter 2

Orientation

"And they will call him Immanuel."
— Matthew 1:23

A Gospel for a Community in Transition

Matthew's Gospel was almost certainly composed in the second half of the first century, most likely in the 80s CE, by a Jewish Christian author writing for a community navigating a significant moment of transition. The destruction of Jerusalem and the Temple in 70 CE had profoundly disrupted Jewish life, and communities that claimed Jesus as Messiah were increasingly distinguishing themselves from the broader Jewish world even as many remained deeply embedded within Jewish culture, Scripture, and practice.

This context shapes the Gospel throughout. Matthew's author is deeply conversant with the Hebrew Bible and rabbinic interpretive traditions. The Gospel's concern with the law, its sustained engagement with the Pharisaic tradition, and its careful attention to Jesus' teaching as a new framework for understanding covenant faithfulness all reflect a community for whom these questions were not abstract but immediately practical. At the same time, Matthew's repeated inclusion of Gentiles — in the genealogy, the visit of the Magi, several healing narratives, and most explicitly in the Great Commission — indicates a community that understood its mission to extend beyond the boundaries of Israel.

The fall of Jerusalem was not an abstract historical event for Jewish Christians living in its aftermath. It was the collapse of the physical and institutional center that had organized their understanding of covenant, worship, and national identity for centuries. The Temple had been the place where heaven and earth met, where sacrifice was offered, where the great festivals gathered the scattered people into visible unity. Its destruction raised urgent questions: What did it mean to be the people of God when the place of God's dwelling had been reduced to rubble? How was atonement to be understood when the sacrificial system was no longer operative? Where was the presence of God to be found now?

Matthew's Gospel addresses these questions not by discussing them directly but by presenting Jesus as the answer that reframes them. He is Immanuel, God with us — the presence of God no longer confined to a building in Jerusalem but embodied in a person who has promised to remain with his community to the end of the age. He is the one through whom forgiveness is extended, not through the Temple's sacrificial system but through his own death and resurrection. Matthew was written for a community that needed to understand how the story continued after the catastrophe of 70 CE, and its answer is that the story continues through Jesus and in the community that bears his name.

Who Wrote Matthew and When

The Gospel of Matthew is technically anonymous — its author does not identify himself within the text, and the attribution to Matthew the tax collector comes from early church tradition. The earliest explicit attribution appears in Papias of Hierapolis, writing in the early second century, who refers to Matthew composing the oracles in the Hebrew language. The precise meaning of this reference and its relationship to the Greek Gospel we now possess has been debated extensively without reaching a settled conclusion.

What internal evidence makes clear is that the author was a Jewish Christian with extraordinary familiarity with the Hebrew Bible in both its Hebrew and Greek forms, with detailed knowledge of first-century Jewish religious interpretive traditions, and with the pastoral instincts of someone who understood the specific pressures facing the community for which he was writing. The author knew the scribal traditions well enough to engage them with precision, and the concerns of a community that included both Jewish and Gentile members well enough to address both with equal care.

Most scholars place the composition in the decade between 80 and 90 CE. The primary reason for placing it after 70 CE is that Matthew refers to the destruction of Jerusalem in the parable of the wedding banquet as a past event carrying theological weight rather than a future event being predicted. The decade of the 80s also fits the picture of a community that has had time to develop internal structures and to work through initial questions about its relationship to the broader Jewish world, without yet having fully resolved those questions.

The place of composition is uncertain, though Antioch in Syria has been proposed most frequently and defended most persuasively. Antioch was a major center of early Christianity where Jewish and Gentile believers had lived and worshipped together since the earliest decades of the movement, where, according to Acts, followers of Jesus were first called Christians. The questions Matthew addresses most insistently — about the relationship between Jewish tradition and Gentile inclusion, about interpretation of the law in light of Jesus — would have been felt with particular urgency there.

The Structure of the Gospel

Matthew is carefully structured. Its most widely recognized feature is five major discourses — extended blocks of teaching — each concluded by a nearly identical transitional formula: when Jesus had finished saying these things. These five discourses are the Sermon on the Mount (chapters 5–7), the Mission Discourse (chapter 10), the Parables Discourse (chapter 13), the Community Discourse (chapter 18), and the Eschatological Discourse (chapters 24–25).

Scholars have long noted that this fivefold structure evokes the five books of the Torah, suggesting Matthew is presenting Jesus as a new Moses who brings a definitive interpretation of the covenant. This parallel is reinforced by other narrative elements — the flight to Egypt and return, the temptation in the wilderness, the mountain as the site of authoritative teaching — all of which invite comparison with the foundational story of Israel.

But the discourses do not float free of their narrative context. Each is embedded within a narrative section that shapes how the teaching is heard. The Sermon on the Mount follows the account of Jesus' baptism, temptation, and early Galilean ministry — establishing his identity before elaborating his teaching. The Eschatological Discourse comes just before the Passion narrative — giving the community its framework for understanding loss and waiting before the story of betrayal, death, and resurrection unfolds.

The five-discourse structure works alongside a broader narrative arc moving through four phases. Chapters 1–4 establish Jesus' identity through the infancy narrative, baptism, and temptation. Chapters 5–13 present the Galilean ministry in full, including the first three discourses and the growing controversy with religious authorities. Chapters 14–20 trace a period of withdrawal and intensified instruction as Jesus moves toward Jerusalem. Chapters 21–28 narrate the Jerusalem ministry, the Passion, and the resurrection.

The placement of each discourse within this arc is deliberate. The Mission Discourse follows Jesus' own ministry of proclamation and healing — the disciples are sent to extend a ministry they have already witnessed. The Parables Discourse follows the intensifying controversy with religious authorities — the turn to speaking in parables is directly connected to the divided response Jesus is encountering. The Community Discourse follows Peter's confession at Caesarea Philippi — it describes the shape of the community that will carry forward the mission of the one whose identity has just been most explicitly revealed. In each case, discourse and narrative illuminate each other, and neither can be fully understood without the other.

Matthew's Sources

Matthew does not appear to have been written without reference to earlier sources. The most widely accepted explanation for the similarities and differences between Matthew, Mark, and Luke holds that Matthew and Luke both drew on two primary sources: the Gospel of Mark, which Matthew follows in narrative sequence while often expanding or modifying its content, and a collection of Jesus' sayings scholars designate Q. This two-source hypothesis accounts for the material Matthew shares with Mark, the material Matthew shares with Luke that is not in Mark, and the significant material unique to Matthew alone.

Matthew is not simply transcribing received tradition. He is interpreting it, organizing it, and shaping it in light of the theological argument he is making and the pastoral needs of the community he is addressing. Where Matthew expands a Markan narrative — adding a teaching section, extending a dialogue, or making an Old Testament connection explicit — the expansion serves a purpose that can usually be identified by reading it in light of Matthew's larger concerns.

The material unique to Matthew includes some of its most theologically central passages: the infancy narrative with the Magi and the flight to Egypt, the Sermon on the Mount in its full form, the parables of the workers in the vineyard, the ten virgins, and the sheep and the goats, the extended woes against the scribes and Pharisees, Peter walking on water. These are not peripheral to Matthew's concerns — they are among the most distinctively Matthean passages in the Gospel.

Matthew's Jesus

Matthew presents Jesus through a cluster of titles that together form a coherent Christological portrait. He is the Messiah, the son of David, who fulfills the covenant promises. He is Immanuel, God with us, the presence of the divine in human form. He is the Son of God, confirmed at his baptism, tested in the wilderness, and confessed at the foot of the cross by a Roman centurion. He is the Son of Man, drawn from Daniel's vision, whose authority holds together both the humble, suffering present and the glorious, authoritative coming.

These titles are not merely honorific. Each carries a freight of scriptural meaning that Matthew's readers, steeped in the Hebrew Bible, would have recognized immediately. The Son of David title was a messianic designation, and Matthew's genealogy establishes it from the first verse. It reappears at key moments throughout the Gospel — when blind men cry out for healing, when crowds wonder whether Jesus might be the Son of David, when children shout hosannas in the Temple. Matthew is making sure readers understand Jesus' ministry within the framework of Israel's royal messianic hope, even as he simultaneously redefines what that hope means.

The Son of Man title functions to hold together two dimensions of Jesus' existence that might otherwise seem contradictory. The Son of Man has nowhere to lay his head and is handed over to be crucified. The Son of Man will also come on the clouds of heaven with power and great glory. Matthew uses this title to prevent readers from separating the humble, suffering, present Jesus from the glorious, authoritative, coming Jesus. They

18

are the same person, and the full picture requires holding both dimensions together.

Matthew's Jesus is also distinctively demanding. The Sermon on the Mount does not lower the bar of covenant faithfulness — it raises it from outward compliance to inward transformation. Following Jesus in Matthew is not primarily a matter of intellectual assent to theological claims. It requires a reorientation of the whole self.

The Role of the Old Testament

No feature of Matthew is more consistently visible than its engagement with the Hebrew Bible. The Gospel contains more explicit quotations from and allusions to Old Testament texts than any other Gospel — many introduced with the formula this was to fulfill what was spoken through the prophet. These formula quotations are structural arguments, placed at decisive moments to interpret what is happening in light of what was promised.

Matthew's interpretive method is not simply proof-texting. It is a more holistic engagement with the story of Israel, in which patterns, types, and trajectories of meaning are identified and shown to find their completion in the story of Jesus. Matthew reads the Hebrew Bible not as a collection of predictions that happen to have come true but as a unified narrative whose inner logic points toward the one who fulfills it.

The formula quotations appear at moments Matthew identifies as decisive. The birth in Bethlehem fulfills Micah's prophecy of the ruler who would come from there. The flight to Egypt and return fulfills Hosea's words about God calling his son out of Egypt — words that originally referred to Israel's Exodus, but that Matthew reads as pointing forward to the one who recapitulates Israel's experience in his own. Each connection claims that the event in question is the moment toward which the ancient text was always pointing.

Matthew's method is about the nature of a story whose ending gives new meaning to everything that preceded it — the way knowing how a story concludes changes the way you read its earlier chapters, revealing significance in details that seemed incidental before the ending made clear what they were building toward. Matthew reads the Hebrew Bible as a story whose ending is Jesus, and reading it that way, he finds that the story is more coherent and more deeply meaningful than it could appear before the ending arrived.

Poetry and Artistry in Matthew

Matthew is not merely a theological document. It is also a literary achievement, and attending to its literary qualities is essential to understanding what it is doing. The Gospel is written with care for language, structure, narrative rhythm, and the ways in which literary form can accomplish theological work that explicit statement cannot.

The genealogy that opens the Gospel is not merely a list of names but a structured argument about the shape of history, organized around significant numbers and figures to convey a claim about Jesus' place in that history before a word of narrative has been spoken. The Sermon on the Mount achieves its effects through the accumulation of parallel structures — the repeated you have heard that it was said, but I say to you of the antitheses — creating a cumulative rhetorical force far greater than any individual statement could produce alone.

Matthew's use of inclusio — beginning and ending a section with the same phrase or image — is especially characteristic. The Gospel opens with the announcement of Immanuel, God with us, and closes with Jesus' promise to be with his disciples to the end of the age, bracketing the entire narrative within the same theme of divine presence. These structural choices are not accidents of composition. They are deliberate literary decisions that shape how the whole is understood.

Preparing to Read Matthew Well

Understanding the historical context of Matthew's composition, the community for which it was written, the sources the author drew upon, the structural features that organize its argument, the portrait of Jesus developed through its cluster of titles, and the method of Old Testament interpretation that runs throughout: all of these are forms of orientation that prepare the reader to engage the text itself more fully.

But orientation is preparation, not replacement. The goal of everything this chapter has described is to remove the obstacles that can prevent a modern reader from engaging Matthew directly — the sense that the historical world is too remote to enter, that the literary structure is too complex to navigate, that the theological claims are too unfamiliar to evaluate honestly. When those obstacles are cleared, what remains is the text itself: a carefully constructed, pastorally intelligent, theologically serious engagement with the question of who Jesus is and what his coming means for those who receive it.

Matthew rewards the reader who brings sustained, attentive, humble engagement. Its depth does not exhaust itself on a single reading. The reader who returns to it, who allows later chapters to illuminate earlier ones, who brings questions generated by experience to texts that seemed settled, will consistently find that Matthew has more to say than any previous reading has fully drawn out.

Chapter 3

The World Behind the Book

*"After Jesus was born in Bethlehem in Judea, during the time of
King Herod, Magi from the east came to Jerusalem and asked,
'Where is the one who has been born king of the Jews?'"*
— Matthew 2:1–2

Roman Judea and the World Jesus Inhabited

The world into which Jesus was born was shaped by the weight of
Roman imperial power on one side and the rich texture of Jewish
religious life on the other. The Roman Empire provided the
administrative framework within which daily life was organized —
taxation, military presence, legal structures, and the infrastructure
of roads and cities that connected the Mediterranean world. But
for the Jewish population of Judea and Galilee, the more
immediate context was Torah observance, the synagogue as a
center of community life, and the memory of the Temple as the
focal point of national worship and identity.

Herod the Great, who ruled as a client king under Roman
authority until his death around 4 BCE, had rebuilt the Temple on
a magnificent scale — a project that physically dominated
Jerusalem and symbolically represented the intersection of Jewish
identity with the realities of a world organized around foreign
power. His successors divided his territory among themselves, and
Roman governors were eventually installed to manage Judea
directly. This political arrangement — Jewish cultural and religious
institutions operating within a framework of Roman sovereignty
— created the specific tensions that run through Matthew's
narrative.

Rome generally permitted subject peoples to maintain their traditional religious practices as long as those practices did not threaten public order. Jews were formally granted exemptions from participation in the imperial cult that most subject peoples were expected to observe, an acknowledgment of the practical difficulty of requiring a people defined by exclusive loyalty to the God of Israel to offer worship to human rulers. But the accommodation was always provisional. The question of taxation was a persistent source of tension — not only because it was economically burdensome for a largely agricultural population operating near subsistence level, but because paying taxes to Caesar with coins bearing his image and inscriptions attributing divine status to him was, for many Jews, a form of participation in the ideological claims of the empire that their theological convictions made deeply uncomfortable. The question posed to Jesus about whether it was lawful to pay taxes to Caesar reflects how charged this issue was.

The physical presence of Roman military forces was another constant reminder of the community's subordination — soldiers stationed throughout Judea and Galilee, the experience of being compelled to carry a soldier's pack for a mile, the knowledge that crucifixion awaited those who challenged imperial power too directly. When Jesus speaks of turning the other cheek and going the extra mile, he is addressing people who know precisely what those situations look like in practice.

The Economic Landscape

The economic conditions of first-century Judea and Galilee were shaped by Roman taxation, Herodian building projects, Temple obligations, and the fundamental realities of an agrarian economy in which most people lived close to the margins of subsistence. The burden of taxation was layered and cumulative — Roman taxes on land, produce, and commerce imposed on top of the

Temple tax and the tithes Torah required on agricultural produce. For the majority of the population, the total burden was substantial and the margin between adequate provision and genuine hardship was narrow.

This economic context is directly relevant to Matthew's narrative in ways easy to underestimate if the text is read without it. The crowds of sick, poor, and marginalized people who gather around Jesus are not background scenery. They are the economic casualties of a system that extracted resources from the bottom of the social hierarchy to support the building projects, military apparatus, and lifestyle of those at the top. The tax collectors who appear repeatedly in Matthew were figures of particular contempt precisely because they were Jewish men who had chosen to work within the Roman system of extraction, collecting taxes from their own people on behalf of the occupying power.

The call of Matthew in chapter nine is therefore a sharply pointed social statement. Jesus calling a tax collector to follow him and then eating with tax collectors and sinners is not merely an expression of personal generosity. It is a deliberate crossing of the social boundaries that the economic system had created and that the respectable community policed carefully. The Pharisees' question — why does your teacher eat with tax collectors and sinners? — reflects the genuine scandal that Jesus' table fellowship represented in a world where eating together expressed and reinforced social solidarity, and where eating with the wrong people was understood as a statement about one's own place in the social order.

The economic dimension of Matthew's narrative becomes most explicit in the parables, many of which are set in the world of agricultural labor, debt, wage negotiation, and financial management, immediately recognizable to Matthew's first readers. The parable of the unforgiving servant involves sums so large the contrast borders on the comic, but the social reality it reflects — debt relationships that bound people to those above them in the economic hierarchy with few means of escape — was anything but comic for those who lived within it. The parable of the workers in the vineyard engages directly with the day-labor system in which agricultural workers gathered each morning hoping to be hired, with no guarantee of work and the constant possibility of ending the day without wages.

The World of the Synagogue

By the first century, the synagogue had become the primary institution of Jewish communal life outside Jerusalem — a place of study and prayer, a center for community gathering, and the setting in which Torah was read and interpreted week by week. The scribes and Pharisees who appear throughout Matthew's Gospel were the recognized authorities in this setting, whose expertise in the interpretation and application of Torah gave them significant social and religious standing.

Matthew's Jesus is repeatedly portrayed as teaching in the synagogues of Galilee, and the conflict that develops between Jesus and the Pharisaic tradition is shaped by this shared institutional context. Both were operating within the same religious world, appealing to the same scriptural tradition, and competing for the loyalty of the same communities. The intensity of the controversy in Matthew reflects how closely the positions were defined against each other — the disagreements were not between strangers but between people who shared much and diverged significantly at precisely the points that mattered most.

The tension between Jesus and the scribes and Pharisees is not simply a conflict between competing ideas. It is a conflict over authority — over who has the right to interpret the community's foundational documents and to define the shape of faithful covenant life. When Jesus teaches in the synagogues with an authority the crowds recognize as different from that of the scribes, he is not merely offering a more interesting theological perspective. He is making a claim that the existing structure of the synagogue did not accommodate and that its existing authorities experienced as a direct challenge to their own standing and legitimacy.

The Pharisees and Their World

The Pharisees deserve more careful attention than they typically receive in popular readings of Matthew, because understanding them accurately is essential to understanding what Matthew's account of Jesus' controversy with them is actually about. The Pharisees have suffered in the popular imagination from centuries of being read primarily through the lens of the Gospel controversies, producing a caricature of smug, hypocritical, legalistic religious professionals. This caricature is historically inaccurate and theologically unhelpful.

The Pharisaic movement was a renewal movement within Judaism, defined by a genuine and serious commitment to the practice of Torah in its fullest form. Their foundational conviction was that the holiness required of the covenant people was not confined to the Temple and its priesthood but extended to every Jewish home and every dimension of daily life. Every meal could be eaten in a state of purity appropriate to the priest at the altar. Every aspect of daily life — food, dress, commerce, family relationships, social interaction — could be shaped by the covenant obligations God had given Israel as the framework of faithful living.

This vision of total covenant faithfulness was genuinely inspiring to many first-century Jews, and the Pharisees' commitment to living it out with consistency and rigor earned them considerable respect. They were not cynics performing a religion they did not believe. Many were deeply sincere people whose religious lives were shaped by genuine conviction. The problem Matthew's Jesus identifies is not hypocrisy in the simple sense of knowing one thing and doing another. It is something more subtle: the tendency of a highly developed system of religious practice to become an end in itself, generating its own internal standards of success and failure that can substitute for the deeper transformation of the person that the practice was originally designed to produce.

Messianic Expectation in First-Century Judaism

The first century was a period of intense messianic expectation. The combination of Roman occupation, economic pressure, and the memory of past deliverances created a climate in which the hope for God's definitive intervention was not merely a theological abstraction but a living social force. Different groups within Judaism held different versions of this expectation — some emphasized military deliverance, others priestly restoration, others the arrival of an anointed figure who would renew the covenant.

The expectation of a royal Davidic Messiah — a king who would restore the monarchy, defeat the occupying powers, and reestablish Israel's sovereignty under God's rule — drew on the royal psalms and the prophetic promises to the Davidic line and had deep roots in the popular religious imagination. This expectation tended toward the political and military in its practical expression. A different strand focused on priestly renewal — a figure who would purify the Temple and restore the proper relationship between Israel and God through properly ordered sacrifice and priestly service. Still other forms of expectation focused less on a specific individual figure and more on direct divine intervention that would transform the cosmic order entirely — the resurrection of the dead, the final judgment, the renewal of creation. This more apocalyptic form of expectation drew on texts like Daniel and was widely represented in first-century Judaism, including among the Pharisees.

Matthew presents a Messiah who simultaneously engages all of these expectations and transcends them all. Jesus is the son of David — the genealogy establishes this from the first verse. But he is not a military or political messiah. He is a priestly figure in the sense that his death accomplishes what Temple sacrifice was designed to produce but could not fully achieve. He inaugurates the renewal of creation in the healings and the resurrection. He gathers the scattered, but the gathering extends beyond Israel to all nations. He is everything the expectations were reaching toward, and more than any single version of those expectations could contain. The distance between expectation and fulfillment is itself one of Matthew's central subjects — visible in the royal entry into Jerusalem on a donkey, in the rejection of political power in the temptation narrative, in the Passion as the climax of the story.

The Experience of Exile and Restoration

Running beneath the surface of Matthew's narrative is the longer story of Israel's experience of exile and incomplete restoration. The return from Babylon in the sixth century BCE had not produced the full renewal the prophets had announced. The Temple had been rebuilt but the Davidic monarchy had not been restored. The nation remained subject to foreign powers. The prophetic promises of a new covenant, a gathered people, a transformed creation — these had been spoken but not yet visibly fulfilled.

In an important sense, many first-century Jews understood themselves as still living in a kind of extended exile. The conditions the prophets had associated with full restoration had not materialized. The Davidic throne was empty. The great ingathering of scattered people from every nation had not occurred. The Spirit had not been poured out in the transforming way the prophets had promised. The new covenant written on the heart rather than on stone had not yet been established. This sense of ongoing or incomplete exile gave particular urgency to prophetic promises that spoke of its definitive end — texts like Isaiah 40–55, with their vision of a new Exodus more glorious than the first, a servant who would bear the sins of many, a renewed covenant more durable than the Mosaic one.

Matthew presents Jesus as the one in whom this larger story reaches its decisive turn. The genealogy is structured to highlight three phases — from Abraham to David, from David to the exile, from the exile to the Messiah — placing Jesus at the end of a long arc of promise and anticipation. Jesus relives the experience of Israel — going down to Egypt and coming out, passing through the waters of the Jordan, spending forty days in the wilderness — not merely as an individual repeating historical patterns but as the one in whom Israel's story is fulfilled and completed. What Israel was called to be and was unable to sustain through its own faithfulness, Jesus embodies fully and permanently. He is the truly faithful Son, where Israel proved repeatedly unfaithful. In him, the story that began with Abraham's call and moved through the covenant at Sinai and the promise to David reaches not merely its continuation but its conclusion.

Daily Life, Household, and Social World

Understanding Matthew's narrative also requires attention to the social world of first-century Galilee and Judea at the level of ordinary daily life. The basic unit of social organization was not the individual but the household — the extended family unit that included parents, children, servants, and dependent relatives, organized around the economic activity of a farm or a trade, and functioning as the primary setting for education, religious formation, and the transmission of cultural identity.

The social world of first-century Palestine was also deeply shaped by the values of honor and shame that governed public reputation across the Mediterranean world. Honor was the most valued social commodity — the public recognition of a person's worth and standing in the community, essential to their ability to function effectively in economic, legal, and social relationships. Many of the social dynamics that shape Matthew's narrative make more sense when read against this background. The public confrontations between Jesus and the religious authorities are not merely theological debates. They are honor contests in which each party is trying to demonstrate publicly that their position is correct and to expose the inadequacy of the other's, with the watching crowds as the audience whose judgment determines the outcome.

Jewish religious life in the first century was organized around practices that gave it its distinctive character. Torah study was central — regular engagement with the written text of Scripture and the oral traditions of interpretation that had developed around it. Prayer was practiced three times daily, oriented toward Jerusalem. The Sabbath structured the week and provided the regular rhythm of cessation from labor that was itself a form of theological statement about the nature of time and human existence. The festivals that marked the Jewish calendar — Passover, Pentecost, Tabernacles — gathered the community into its shared narrative and gave regular expression to the corporate memory and hope that sustained Jewish identity across generations. All of these practices appear in Matthew's narrative in ways that reveal both their importance and the questions Jesus' teaching and practice raised about their proper understanding.

A World Defined by Hope

The world behind Matthew is finally a world defined by hope — a hope tested by centuries of disappointment without being extinguished, refined by the experience of exile and partial restoration into something more honest and more searching than the unreflective optimism that precedes genuine suffering. The prophets who sustained Israel through the Babylonian exile did not minimize the reality of what had happened or offer easy assurances. They engaged honestly with the catastrophe and found within it, through sustained engagement with the character of the God who had called Israel into existence, the grounds of a hope more durable than any that circumstances could provide or remove.

Matthew's Gospel inhabits this same posture. It is written for a community that knows something of loss — the loss of the Temple, the disruption of familiar structures, the increasing pressure of living as a minority community within a majority culture that does not share its convictions. It does not offer easy comfort or quick resolution. It presents a Messiah who accomplished his mission through suffering and death, a community promised persecution along with blessing, and a future that is certain, but whose fullness has not yet arrived. This is the world behind the book — not a world of triumphant certainty but a world of tested hope, sustained by the conviction that the God who had kept every previous promise would keep this one too.

Chapter 4

The Story or Flow of the Book

*"From that time on, Jesus began to preach, 'Repent, for the
kingdom of heaven has come near.'"*
— Matthew 4:17

The Shape of Matthew's Narrative

Matthew unfolds in a movement that is both narratively
compelling and theologically purposeful. It begins with the
establishment of Jesus' identity — through his genealogy, birth,
the visit of the Magi, his baptism, and his temptation. It moves
through an extended period of ministry in Galilee marked by
teaching, healing, and growing controversy. It then turns
decisively toward Jerusalem, where the confrontation between
Jesus and the religious authorities reaches its climax in the Passion
narrative. And it concludes with the resurrection and the
commissioning of the disciples.

This movement is not simply chronological. Matthew shapes
his material to develop a cumulative argument about who Jesus is
and what his coming means. The five great discourses anchor the
narrative at key points, and the controversies that intensify as the
Gospel progresses reveal both the claims Jesus is making and the
resistance those claims provoke.

Matthew is not simply recording what happened. He is
interpreting what happened, and the interpretation is woven into
the narrative at every level. The formula quotations throughout
the Gospel are the most visible expression of this interpretive
activity, but they are far from the only one. The selection of which
miracles to include, the arrangement of controversies in sequences
that build toward crisis, the placement of each discourse within

the narrative context that gives it its proper frame of reference: all of these are interpretive decisions that reflect Matthew's sustained effort to help readers understand not merely what happened but what it means.

The Structure of the Whole

Matthew can be understood as organized around four major phases. The first, covering chapters 1–4, establishes the identity of Jesus before his public ministry begins. The second, chapters 5–13, presents the Galilean ministry in its fullest form, including the first three great discourses and the growing controversy with the religious authorities. The third, chapters 14–20, traces a period of withdrawal from public ministry and intensive formation of the disciples as Jesus moves toward Jerusalem. The fourth, chapters 21–28, narrates the Jerusalem ministry, the Passion, and the resurrection.

Within this four-phase structure, the five discourses serve as the organizing backbone of the teaching material. The Sermon on the Mount establishes the character of kingdom life at the beginning of Jesus' public teaching. The Mission Discourse sends the disciples to extend the ministry they have witnessed. The Parables Discourse interprets the divided response to Jesus' ministry. The Community Discourse describes the shape of the community that will carry the mission forward. The Eschatological Discourse provides the framework within which the community understands its situation between Jesus' departure and his return. Together, these five discourses provide the theological content that the narrative develops and demonstrates, and each is carefully positioned so that its narrative context shapes how the teaching is heard.

Preparation and Announcement

The opening two chapters establish the identity and context of Jesus before he speaks a word. The genealogy traces his lineage through the covenantal figures of Israel's history, organized into three groups of fourteen generations — from Abraham to David, from David to the exile, from the exile to the Messiah — placing Jesus at the culminating point of a long and purposeful history. Four women are included in the genealogy — Tamar, Rahab, Ruth, and the wife of Uriah — not because they are the most prominent female ancestors available, but because each is a figure through whom God worked in ways that were unexpected or socially unconventional. Their inclusion signals from the beginning that the story Matthew is telling will consistently confound ordinary expectations about where God's activity is to be found.

The birth narrative is structured around five formula quotations connecting events to specific Old Testament texts. Matthew is not claiming that each prophet consciously predicted these specific events. He is claiming something more complex: that the story of Jesus is the story toward which the entire narrative of Israel was always moving, and that reading Israel's story with this ending in view reveals dimensions of meaning that could not be seen before the ending arrived.

The Magi who arrive from the east establish a pattern that will recur throughout the Gospel: outsiders who recognize what insiders miss. They travel a great distance to worship the one born king of the Jews, while Herod responds with the violence of threatened power, and the chief priests and scribes — who know the relevant prophecy precisely — show no interest in investigating whether it has been fulfilled. The alignment of recognizing faith with the unexpected and of resistance with the established is not accidental. It is the pattern Matthew will develop throughout the narrative of Jesus' ministry.

The baptism of Jesus identifies him simultaneously as the promised royal Messiah and the suffering servant — by combining allusions to Psalm 2 and Isaiah 42 in the divine voice's single declaration. These were two figures many in Israel had not expected to be the same person. The temptation narrative that follows tests that identity through three structured challenges: if you are the Son of God, do this or that. Each offers Jesus a way of exercising his messianic role that would bypass the cross. Jesus refuses all three with words drawn from Deuteronomy, demonstrating that he is the truly obedient Son that Israel was called to be but repeatedly failed to become.

The Galilean Ministry

The Sermon on the Mount in chapters 5–7 is the defining document of the Galilean ministry. Its Beatitudes are not a list of virtues to be cultivated, but announcements — declarations about a new state of affairs the kingdom's arrival is bringing into being. The poor in spirit, the mourning, the meek, those who hunger and thirst for righteousness: these are people in conditions of need and longing, not people who have achieved a desirable spiritual state. The kingdom of heaven belongs to them not because their condition is admirable but because the arrival of the kingdom addresses precisely the conditions from which they suffer.

The six antitheses — you have heard that it was said, but I say to you — represent one of the most significant moments in the entire Gospel. Jesus takes six commandments from the Torah and deepens their demand by tracing the prohibited behavior back to its interior root. Do not murder becomes do not be angry. Do not commit adultery becomes do not look at a woman with lust. These are not simply more stringent versions of the same requirements. They represent a fundamental reconception of what righteousness demands: not the regulation of outward behavior but the transformation of the interior life from which behavior grows.

The teaching on piety in chapter 6 addresses the same interior-exterior distinction from a different angle. The issue is not whether almsgiving, prayer, and fasting are performed but why and for whom. To perform them in order to be seen is to have received one's reward already. The Lord's Prayer embedded in this section provides a model that expresses the proper orientation of the one who prays: toward God as Father, toward the kingdom as the primary reality, toward daily dependence and mutual forgiveness as the texture of life within the kingdom community.

The call narratives that punctuate the early chapters have a quality of compressed drama. When Jesus calls Simon and Andrew, at once they left their nets and followed him. The narrative refuses to slow down for psychological explanation because the point is not their psychology but the authority of the one who calls and the adequacy of that authority to produce an immediate, total response. The call of Matthew the tax collector is followed by a scene of table fellowship with tax collectors and sinners that provokes the Pharisees' question: why does your teacher eat with tax collectors and sinners? Jesus' answer — I have not come to call the righteous but sinners — is not simply a defense of his table companions. It is a statement about the nature of the mission he has come to accomplish.

Controversy and Turning Point

Chapters 11 and 12 mark a decisive turn in the narrative — a gathering of controversies about Sabbath observance, accusations of demonic power, and demands for signs that reveal the intensifying opposition. The accusation that Jesus casts out demons by Beelzebul represents an escalation into different territory: the Pharisees are not merely disagreeing with his interpretation of the Sabbath but attributing his power to the most malevolent possible source. Jesus' counter-claim is more alarming than the accusation: if he casts out demons by the Spirit of God, then the kingdom of God has come upon them. The refusal to recognize it is the most serious possible form of resistance.

The parable discourse of chapter 13 follows immediately, and the shift to speaking in parables is explicitly connected to this divided response. The parable of the sower observes that different kinds of soil respond differently to the same seed and invites the hearer to ask which kind they represent. The parable of the weeds alongside the wheat resists the impulse to purify the community prematurely — the sorting will happen at the harvest, not before. The parables of the mustard seed and the yeast affirm the ultimate scope of the kingdom's growth from unpromising beginnings. The parables of hidden treasure and the pearl insist on the surpassing value of the kingdom that justifies any cost of acquisition. The parables do not explain why the kingdom meets divided reception. They invite sustained reflection on its nature.

The Journey Toward Jerusalem

Chapters 14–20 trace a period of intensified instruction of the disciples as Jesus moves progressively toward Jerusalem. The feeding of the five thousand is narrated with deliberate echoes of Israel's feeding in the wilderness, and the sequence — taking bread, looking up to heaven, giving thanks, breaking, distributing — will later be recognized as the pattern of the Eucharist.

Peter's walking on the water is a compressed portrait of discipleship in its characteristic form: genuine faith, genuine fear, sinking, and rescue. Jesus reaches toward those who are sinking not as a reward for adequate faith but as the consistent expression of his willingness to help regardless of the adequacy of their faith.

Peter's confession at Caesarea Philippi — you are the Messiah, the Son of the living God — is the central turning point of the disciples' formation. But the confession is immediately followed by the first explicit passion prediction, and Peter's response reveals how partial his understanding remains. When Jesus declares that the Son of Man must suffer and be killed, Peter rebukes him. He has grasped the title without grasping its content — without understanding that the Messiah must suffer before he is glorified. Jesus' response — get behind me, Satan — reflects how serious the misunderstanding is. To refuse the cross is to refuse the very thing that makes the kingdom possible.

Jerusalem and the Passion

The entry into Jerusalem is staged with careful attention to Zechariah's prophecy of a king coming humbly and mounted on a donkey. The choice of an animal associated with peace rather than a warhorse associated with military triumph is deliberate. The triumphal entry is not a triumphal entry in any ordinary sense. It is the arrival of a king whose kingship will be exercised through suffering and death rather than conquest and dominion.

The cleansing of the Temple immediately follows, framing everything after it as an assertion of prophetic authority over an institution that has failed its proper purpose. The blind and the lame who come to Jesus in the Temple, and the children who cry Hosanna — figures who would normally have been excluded — are welcomed and healed. The proper order of the Temple is being enacted even as the corrupt version is being challenged.

The extended controversies of chapters 21–23 represent a sustained public confrontation between Jesus and the full range of Jerusalem's religious establishment. By the end, the religious authorities have been silenced, and the stage has been set for the woes of chapter 23 that represent the climax of Matthew's critique of the scribal and Pharisaic tradition.

The Gethsemane account is among the most moving passages in the entire Gospel. My soul is overwhelmed with sorrow to the point of death. Jesus prays three times, asking that the cup be taken from him, submitting each time to the Father's will. The three prayers and the three sleeping disciples form a deliberate contrast: Jesus moves through genuine anguish to genuine acceptance, while those who promised to stay awake cannot manage even that. The acceptance Jesus reaches is not the acceptance of someone who has stopped feeling the weight of what is coming. It is the acceptance of someone who has felt that weight fully and chosen, in full awareness of what it means, to trust the Father's will.

The resurrection narrative in chapter 28 is brief but consequential. The women who come to the tomb are the first witnesses. The risen Jesus commissions his disciples with words that give the Great Commission its double claim: all authority and all nations. The ending of Matthew is not a conclusion but a launching point — the story continues beyond the pages of the book in the mission it commissions.

The Meaning of the Whole

Reading Matthew's narrative from beginning to end — attending to the way each section develops from what has preceded it and prepares for what follows, the way the discourses illuminate the narrative and the narrative gives the discourses their context, the way the controversies intensify toward a crisis that the Passion represents and the resurrection resolves — produces an understanding of the whole that is qualitatively different from anything achieved by engaging individual passages in isolation.

Matthew is a carefully crafted argument about the identity and significance of Jesus, made through narrative rather than through systematic theology. Its claim is that in this specific person, at this specific moment in the long story of God's dealings with Israel, something has happened that changes everything — that the kingdom of heaven has arrived, the promises of the prophets have been fulfilled, and the death and resurrection of

Jesus are the hinge events of human history. These claims are not stated once and left at that. They are developed and pressed home from every angle across the entire narrative, each episode contributing something to the cumulative case the whole is building. The story Matthew tells is the argument Matthew makes, and understanding the argument requires following the story all the way through.

Chapter 5

Key Themes

"Blessed are the poor in spirit, for theirs is the kingdom of heaven."
— *Matthew 5:3*

The Kingdom of Heaven

No theme is more central to Matthew's Gospel than the kingdom of heaven. The phrase appears more than fifty times — more frequently than in any other Gospel — and it functions as the organizing category for nearly everything Jesus teaches and does.

The kingdom of heaven is not primarily a place. It is a state of affairs — the active reign of God breaking into the present order of things. When Jesus announces that the kingdom of heaven has come near, he is declaring that what God has always been moving toward is now arriving in tangible, historically specific form. The healings demonstrate it, the teaching articulates its character, the community of disciples embodies it, and the death and resurrection bring it to its decisive establishment.

Matthew's kingdom is both present and future. It arrives with Jesus, but it is not yet fully realized. The parables of chapter thirteen capture this tension: the kingdom is like a mustard seed, small now, but growing toward something vast. It is like yeast, hidden at work within the whole. It is like a treasure or a pearl, demanding total reorientation because it is worth more than everything else. The kingdom is here and coming; it has arrived and is not yet complete. The community that forms around Jesus is the community that lives within this tension — already receiving the kingdom's gifts and already called to embody its values, while waiting for its completion. This is not a comfortable position, and Matthew does not pretend that it is. It is the genuine situation of the community of faith in every era.

Matthew's preference for heaven rather than God reflects the characteristic Jewish practice of avoiding direct use of the divine name — for Matthew's Jewish Christian readers, the phrase carried exactly the weight that kingdom of God carries in the other Gospels, with appropriate reverential restraint.

The Costliness of the Kingdom

The parables of the hidden treasure and the pearl of great price describe the discovery of the kingdom in terms that emphasize its surpassing value and the total response that value demands. A man finds treasure hidden in a field and in his joy sells everything he has and buys that field. A merchant finds a pearl of great value and sells everything he has to buy it. The details are spare to the point of being skeletal — no background, no psychological development, no account of consequences. The entire focus falls on the single act of total divestiture in response to a discovery of surpassing worth.

These parables are about the actual reordering of priorities that the kingdom's arrival requires — the practical, costly, concrete reorganization of one's life around a new center of gravity that displaces every other organizing principle. The rich young man in chapter nineteen comes to Jesus asking what he must do to inherit eternal life, and after confirming that he has kept the commandments from his youth, Jesus tells him that the one thing he lacks is the willingness to sell his possessions, give to the poor, and follow. The young man goes away sorrowful because he has great possessions. Matthew does not soften this outcome. The kingdom makes demands that are genuinely costly, and the costliness reflects its insistence on being the organizing center of a life rather than an addition to a life organized around other centers.

Fulfillment of Scripture

Matthew's sustained engagement with the Hebrew Bible is a theological claim: the story of Jesus is the story toward which the entire history of God's dealings with Israel has been moving. The formula quotations at key moments throughout the narrative are the most visible expression of this claim, but the deeper engagement runs throughout — in the typological parallels with Moses, in the five discourses echoing the Torah, in the Passion narrative's resonance with the Psalms of lament and the Servant Songs of Isaiah.

Matthew reads the Hebrew Bible as a living narrative whose patterns and trajectories of meaning are genuinely illuminated by — and in turn illuminate — the events of Jesus' life, death, and resurrection. The quotation from Isaiah 7 about a virgin conceiving and bearing a son called Immanuel was originally spoken in the context of a political crisis in eighth-century Judah. Its fulfillment in Jesus is not the fulfillment of what Isaiah was primarily describing in that historical moment. It is the fulfillment of the deeper pattern of divine presence and deliverance that the original sign represented, now achieved in a form far more complete and permanent than any eighth-century political event could have been.

The quotation from Hosea — out of Egypt I called my son — was originally Israel's origin story. Its application to Jesus returning from Egypt claims that the pattern of God's relationship with his son that the Exodus established finds its ultimate expression in Jesus, the truly obedient Son who relives the founding experience of God's people in order to accomplish what that people was called to be but proved unable to sustain.

The five discourses that structure Matthew's teaching evoke the five books of the Torah through structural parallel — the same number of foundational documents, organized around the same authoritative figure, shaping the life of the same covenant community. But Jesus is more than Moses: the one who fulfills what Moses pointed toward. The figure of Moses provides Matthew's most sustained typological parallel. Jesus is endangered in infancy by a ruler who kills children. He is brought out of Egypt and called back. He passes through water, spends forty days in the wilderness, goes up on a mountain to give the authoritative teaching of the new covenant, feeds the multitude in a deserted place. Taken together these parallels are unmistakable — Matthew is presenting Jesus as the new and greater Moses whose arrival the tradition had anticipated.

The Servant Songs of Isaiah provide another sustained point of reference. The baptism account draws on the first Servant Song to identify Jesus as the Servant whose mission those four poems describe. The fourth Servant Song — which describes the Servant's suffering and death as the means by which the sins of many are borne — provides the theological framework within which Matthew presents the Passion. The crucifixion is not simply an execution but the enactment of the Servant's mission, accomplished precisely through the suffering that every version of messianic expectation had found most difficult to accommodate.

Discipleship and the Community of Faith

Matthew's Gospel is distinctively interested in the formation of disciples. The disciples are not idealized figures. They misunderstand, they lose faith, they argue about status, and at the crucial moment of the Passion they abandon and deny Jesus. But they are also the ones to whom the great discourses are addressed, who are sent on mission, and who receive the final commission of the risen Christ.

Matthew's portrait of discipleship is realistic to the point of discomfort. It presents the disciples as people who have received something genuinely transformative and who have not yet been fully transformed by it. The characteristic form of their failure is

the failure of faith in the face of threatening circumstances —
sinking on the water, unable to cast out a demon, fearful in the
storm. The phrase little faith, which Jesus applies to them
repeatedly, is not a judgment that they have no faith but that their
faith is not yet robust enough to sustain itself through the
conditions that reveal its fragility. The pattern of diagnosis and
gentle correction rather than condemnation and dismissal is itself
a portrait of the discipleship relationship.

Chapter 18 is Matthew's most focused treatment of the
community that discipleship creates. The instruction on seeking
the one who has gone astray opens with a parable that establishes
the community's fundamental orientation toward its most
vulnerable members: a man with a hundred sheep leaves the
ninety-nine to seek the one that has strayed. This parable is not
primarily about evangelism. It is about the community's
responsibility for those within it who are in danger of being lost.
The community that allows members to drift away without pursuit
has failed its primary obligation.

The instruction on conflict resolution in chapter 18 describes
a discipline designed to preserve relationship through honest
engagement rather than allowing conflict to fester through
avoidance. When a brother or sister sins against you, go and show
them their fault, just between the two of you. The process only
escalates when the goal of restoration has been genuinely pursued
at simpler levels and has not been achieved. The goal at every
stage is winning the brother or sister, not vindicating oneself.

The teaching on forgiveness that follows — not seven times
but seventy-seven times — is a refusal of calculation. The
community of the kingdom does not count its forgiveness and
stop when a threshold has been reached. The parable of the
unforgiving servant makes the ground of this forgiveness explicit:
the community forgiven an unpayable debt has no legitimate basis
for withholding forgiveness of a manageable one. The failure to

forgive is evidence that the grace one has received has not yet done the transforming work it was designed to do.

Righteousness and the Interior Life

A recurring concern in Matthew is the relationship between outward observance and the inner condition that true righteousness requires. The six antitheses of the Sermon on the Mount trace familiar commandments back to the interior dispositions from which righteous or unrighteous behavior grows. Do not murder becomes do not be angry. Do not commit adultery becomes do not look with lust. The prohibition of false oaths becomes the call for such complete integrity that oaths are unnecessary.

What the antitheses describe is not a more rigorous version of the same approach to righteousness that the scribal tradition employs. They describe a fundamentally different approach — one that addresses the root rather than the fruit, that seeks transformation rather than management, that aims at the formation of a person whose interior life is genuinely aligned with what God requires. This demand cannot be met by trying harder to comply with rules that address outward behavior. It can only be met by a genuine reorientation of the interior life that changes what a person desires, what they fear, and what they are willing to do when no one is watching.

The controversy passages in chapters 12–23 return to this interior-exterior distinction from multiple angles. The challenge about hand-washing in chapter 15 locates the source of defilement precisely in the interior life. The woes of chapter 23 build to the same conclusion: you clean the outside of the cup and dish but inside they are full of greed and self-indulgence. Clean the inside of the cup first, and then the outside also will be clean.

Judgment and Accountability

Matthew's Gospel contains some of the most searching passages about divine judgment in the New Testament. The three eschatological parables of chapter 25 — the ten virgins, the talents, and the sheep and the goats — each address accountability before God in searching and memorable terms.

The parable of the ten virgins addresses the challenge of faithful waiting in conditions of extended uncertainty. All ten virgins have lamps; all ten go out to meet the bridegroom. The division falls not between those who are waiting and those who are not, but between those who have prepared for the waiting to be longer than expected and those who have not. The parable is addressed to communities genuinely waiting for Jesus' return but unprepared for the extended duration that faithfulness will actually require.

The parable of the talents addresses accountability for the use of what has been entrusted. The third servant's justification for burying rather than investing is fear — his assessment of the master as hard and demanding. But the master's response exposes this fear as theologically mistaken: if the master is as demanding as the servant claimed, that is all the more reason to have invested rather than buried. The fear that was supposed to justify inaction actually condemns it, because it reveals a fundamentally distorted understanding of who the master is.

The parable of the sheep and the goats is the most morally searching of the three. The Son of Man separates the nations as a shepherd separates sheep from goats. To those on his right: I was hungry and you gave me something to eat, I was thirsty and you gave me something to drink, I was a stranger and you invited me in. The righteous are astonished — when did we see you in these conditions? And the answer: whatever you did for one of the least of these brothers and sisters of mine, you did for me. The same structure applies in reverse to those on the left. Both groups are equally astonished. Neither knew.

The entire parable turns on the identification of the Son of Man with the vulnerable — the hungry, the thirsty, the stranger, the sick, the imprisoned — an identification so unexpected that neither those who served them nor those who neglected them recognized it as an encounter with Christ. The care of the vulnerable is therefore not merely an ethical obligation. It is a form of encounter with the living Lord, as real and significant as any more explicitly religious form of encounter. Matthew places this at the climax of the Eschatological Discourse — the last major theological point the reader encounters before being brought face to face with the death that gives it its ultimate ground.

The Great Commission and Universal Mission

Matthew's Gospel moves from its most local roots — a genealogy rooted in Abraham, a birth story set in a small Judean town, a ministry concentrated in the villages of Galilee — to its most expansive horizon: all authority in heaven and on earth has been given to me, therefore go and make disciples of all nations. This movement from the particular to the universal is not an afterthought appended to the narrative. It is the destination toward which the entire Gospel has been traveling.

The seeds of this universality are planted from the first pages. The Magi who arrive from the east to worship the child-king are Gentiles, and their recognition of Jesus stands in contrast to the indifference of those who hold Israel's Scriptures. The genealogy itself includes four women — Tamar, Rahab, Ruth, the wife of Uriah — whose presence signals that the story of God's purposes has never been confined to the expected boundaries. When Jesus heals a Roman centurion's servant in chapter eight, he declares that many will come from east and west and take their places at the feast in the kingdom of heaven. The Great Commission at the end of the Gospel is not a reversal of what has come before. It is its fulfillment.

Matthew's formulation of the commission is the most comprehensive in the New Testament. It is grounded in a claim of authority — all authority in heaven and on earth — that is the risen Christ's own claim, not a delegated mandate from a higher power. It is directed to all nations, without qualification or hierarchy. And its content is specified with unusual precision: baptizing and teaching them to obey everything I have commanded you. The commission is not simply to announce the gospel but to form communities shaped by the full scope of what Matthew's Gospel has presented — the Beatitudes, the Sermon on the Mount, the community ethics of chapter eighteen, the care of the vulnerable in chapter twenty-five. Matthew's mission is the reproduction of the whole.

The promise that concludes the commission — I am with you always, to the very end of the age — is the fulfillment of the Immanuel announcement with which the Gospel began. The child named God with us has become the risen Lord who promises never to withdraw that presence from the community he sends. The Great Commission is therefore not a burden to be discharged through human effort. It is an invitation to participate in a work the risen Christ is already doing in the world, sustained by a presence that does not diminish with distance, with difficulty, or with the passage of time.

This theme also carries the weight of Matthew's unresolved tension between Jewish particularity and Gentile inclusion. Throughout the Gospel, Jesus operates primarily within the boundaries of Israel — he is sent to the lost sheep of the house of Israel, and he initially restricts the disciples' mission in the same terms. The Canaanite woman's persistence in chapter fifteen presses against that boundary and receives a response that acknowledges its limits. By the end of the Gospel, those limits have been dissolved entirely. The community that began as a renewal movement within Israel is now commissioned for the whole of humanity. Matthew holds both dimensions without collapsing either, and the Great Commission is where that long-developing tension reaches its resolution.

Chapter 6

Where People Get It Wrong

"Not everyone who says to me, 'Lord, Lord,' will enter the
kingdom of heaven, but only the one who does the will of my Father
who is in heaven."
— Matthew 7:21

Reducing the Sermon on the Mount to Moral Advice

Perhaps the most common misreading of Matthew's Gospel is the reduction of the Sermon on the Mount to an elevated form of moral instruction — a set of challenging ethical ideals that might be admired even by people who make no particular claim about Jesus himself. On this reading, the Beatitudes become noble attitudes to cultivate, and the teachings on anger, lust, and honesty become a demanding but essentially human-scale program for self-improvement.

This reading misses the eschatological grounding of everything the Sermon says. Jesus is not simply a wise teacher offering good advice about how to live. He is the one in whom the kingdom of heaven has arrived, and the Sermon describes the quality of life appropriate to that arrival. The Beatitudes are not instructions about how to achieve the blessed condition — they are announcements of the reversals that the kingdom brings. The commands that follow are not achievable by willpower alone; they require the transforming presence of the one who gives them. The Sermon is not a program for self-improvement. It is a description of what life looks like when it has been genuinely reoriented around Jesus.

This matters practically because it changes the question the Sermon is answering. If the Sermon is universal moral instruction,

the question it answers is: how should I live? If it is kingdom
ethics addressed to the community of disciples, the question is
something closer to: what does life in the kingdom look like for
those who have received it? The first invites people to adopt the
Sermon's teachings as a program for self-improvement. The
second invites people to encounter the one who speaks the
Sermon and to allow that encounter to produce the life it
describes. The first places the burden of implementation entirely
on human effort. The second recognizes that the life the Sermon
describes requires the transformation that relationship with Jesus
makes possible.

The practical consequences are significant. Communities that
read the Sermon as moral advice tend to produce one of two
responses in those who take it seriously: either the pride of those
who believe they are meeting its demands adequately, or the
despair of those who recognize that they are not. Neither response
is the one the Sermon is designed to produce. It is designed to
produce recognition — an honest encounter with the depth of
transformation that the kingdom requires — and, from that
recognition, a turn toward the one who both demands and enables
it. The poverty of spirit that the first Beatitude blesses is the very
condition that the Sermon, honestly read, is meant to produce in
those who hear it.

The Specific Misreading of the Beatitudes

The most persistent misreading of the Beatitudes treats them as
descriptions of virtues to be cultivated — a list of spiritual
attitudes that the kingdom rewards and that disciples should work
to develop. On this reading, poverty of spirit is a form of spiritual
humility achievable through the discipline of recognizing one's
limitations. Mourning is the spiritually productive sorrow over sin
that a serious religious life should include. Meekness is the
cultivated gentleness of the spiritually mature person.

The problem is that this reading turns the Beatitudes inside out. The poor in spirit are not the spiritually humble — they are those who know with genuine honesty that they have nothing to bring to God. The mourning are not those who have achieved a productive spiritual sorrow — they are those who are actually grieving. The meek are not those who have cultivated gentleness as a virtue — they are those who lack the power or status to impose their will on the situations they inhabit.

Matthew's Beatitudes describe people in conditions of genuine need and announce that these are precisely the people to whom the kingdom of heaven comes. The announcement is not that their condition is admirable — poverty of spirit, mourning, and meekness are not comfortable conditions — but that their condition is the condition in which the arrival of the kingdom makes the most difference. This is good news specifically addressed to specific conditions of human need, not a reward system for those who have achieved certain spiritual states.

When the Beatitudes are read as virtues, the Sermon becomes an extended description of the ideal disciple. This reading is not without any merit — the Sermon does describe the character of life in the kingdom. But the function it assigns to the Sermon is fundamentally different from what Matthew intends. The Sermon is designed to do the work of honest confrontation — to address those who hear it at the level of their actual interior life, and to produce the recognition of need that the kingdom's arrival addresses. The Sermon moves toward the poor in spirit rather than away from them.

Treating the Kingdom as Purely Future

A second common misreading treats the kingdom of heaven as an entirely future reality — a state of affairs that will arrive after death or at the end of history, but that has little bearing on the present. This reading is understandable given the genuine future dimension of the kingdom in Matthew, but it fails to account for the present tense of Jesus' announcement: the kingdom of heaven has come near. The healings, the exorcisms, and the gathering of a new community are not merely anticipations of a future reality. They are the actual arrival of that reality in tangible, historical form.

When the kingdom is treated as purely future, Matthew's ethical demands lose their grounding in something real. They float free of the announcement that gives them their context and become simply a demanding code of conduct. Recovering the present dimension of the kingdom restores the connection: the ethics of the Sermon are possible — and called for — because the kingdom has already begun to arrive in the person and ministry of Jesus.

The practical consequences are visible in communities that have made peace with existing social arrangements on the grounds that the kingdom is not a present reality demanding the reordering of present conditions but a future reality whose coming justifies patient acceptance of present ones. Matthew's Jesus, who heals the sick and feeds the hungry and gathers the outcast in concrete demonstrations of the kingdom's present arrival, provides little support for this accommodation. The kingdom he announces is actively transforming the present order of things, and the community that embodies it is called to embody that transformation in the concrete texture of its common life.

The Collapse into Pure Immanence

The opposite error — collapsing the kingdom entirely into the present — is equally distorting. On this reading, the kingdom of heaven is essentially the just ordering of human society, a this-worldly social ideal that followers of Jesus are called to work toward. The kingdom arrives not through divine intervention but through human effort, not as a gift but as an achievement.

Matthew provides little support for this reading. The kingdom is not a social program but a divine reality that arrives from outside the human order and transforms it. The healings are not evidence that human beings are becoming more capable of care but that the power of God is at work in a new way. The resurrection is not a symbol of the persistence of the human spirit but an actual event in which the one who was dead is now alive.

The kingdom of heaven in Matthew is always a gift before it is a calling, always an arrival before it is a task, always a reality the community receives before it is a vision the community pursues. The ethics of the Sermon on the Mount are the ethics of a community that has already received the kingdom. They are not a program for producing the kingdom through moral effort — a distinction that determines the fundamental orientation of the community's life.

Misunderstanding the Law in Matthew

Matthew's relationship to the law has generated misunderstanding in both directions. Some readers take Jesus' statement that he came not to abolish the law but to fulfill it as a simple endorsement of the legal tradition. Others interpret the antitheses of the Sermon as a replacement of the Mosaic tradition with a new and higher code.

Neither reading captures Matthew's actual position. To fulfill the law is not merely to observe it more carefully. It is to bring it to the completion toward which its own internal logic was always pointing — to disclose the full meaning it was designed to carry and to accomplish in one's own person the reality to which it was always pointing forward. The antitheses do not set aside the commandments but radicalize them, tracing their requirements back to their roots in the interior life. Do not murder was always asking for something more than the avoidance of homicide. Its full meaning — which Jesus discloses — is the cultivation of a character in which the anger from which murder grows has been genuinely addressed. Matthew's Jesus is not setting aside the law. He is completing it.

Flattening the Disciples

Matthew's disciples are sometimes read either as models of faithful response — exemplary figures whose immediate obedience is meant to be imitated — or as consistent failures whose lack of understanding makes them cautionary examples. Both readings flatten what is actually a more complex and realistic portrait.

The disciples in Matthew are genuinely called and genuinely responsive. But they are also people of little faith who sink in the waves, argue about status, and scatter at the arrest. Matthew is not presenting ideal disciples for imitation or failed disciples as warnings. It is presenting the community of faith as it actually is — summoned to something beyond itself, genuinely responsive, and regularly failing to live up to what it has been summoned to, yet not abandoned by the one who called it.

The idealization of the disciples produces a picture that is inspirational but ultimately unhelpful, presenting a form of discipleship unlike anything actual communities experience in practice. People who find that their own discipleship involves the same mixture of genuine response and genuine failure that Matthew's disciples display conclude either that something is wrong with their faith specifically, or that Matthew's portrait cannot be honest. Neither conclusion is warranted, but both follow from allowing an idealized reading to define the expectations that real people bring to their own experience of following Jesus.

The phrase little faith — appearing in Matthew more than in any other Gospel — captures the distinction with precision. Little faith is not the absence of faith. It is faith that is genuine but insufficient — faith that holds in favorable conditions but loses its grip when circumstances become threatening. Peter walking on water is the paradigmatic example: genuine faith, genuine action, genuine failure when fear takes over, and immediate rescue. The pattern of diagnosis and gentle correction that follows, rather than condemnation and dismissal, is itself a portrait of the discipleship relationship Matthew is describing.

Reading the Controversies as Anti-Jewish

The intensity of the conflict between Jesus and the religious authorities — particularly the woes of chapter 23 — has sometimes been read as evidence of a fundamentally anti-Jewish stance on Matthew's part. This is a serious misreading with significant consequences for how the Gospel has been used.

Matthew's Gospel is itself a deeply Jewish document, written from within the tradition it critiques. The polemic against the scribes and Pharisees follows a long tradition of prophetic critique within Judaism — a tradition that insisted that authentic covenant faithfulness required more than outward performance. The woes of chapter 23 are not directed at Judaism as such but at a specific pattern of religious practice that mistakes visible performance for genuine righteousness.

The history of the anti-Jewish misreading of Matthew is long and painful, and acknowledging it honestly is a necessary part of engaging with the Gospel responsibly. From the early centuries of the church, Matthew's controversy material has been used to characterize Judaism as a religion of hypocritical legalism and to justify the marginalization of Jewish communities. This history cannot be set aside as the misuse of a text that bears no responsibility for what was done with it.

Acknowledging this history does not require abandoning Matthew or refusing to read its controversy material. It requires reading that material with the care that its history of misappropriation demands — understanding who is speaking, to whom, about what, and in what tradition.

Crucially, the woes are addressed to the scribes and Pharisees but delivered in the hearing of the disciples. They are not primarily a pronouncement of condemnation, but a teaching directed at the community that hears them — a warning about patterns of religious practice available to any religious community in any era. Every one of the seven woes describes a failure available to the community of disciples as surely as it is observable in the scribes and Pharisees. The woes are a mirror, not merely a condemnation of others. The pattern of visible religious performance that substitutes for genuine interior transformation, the accumulation of religious authority used to burden others, the meticulous observance of minor regulations while major justice concerns are neglected: these are not specifically Jewish failures. They are the characteristic failures of religious institutions in general.

Misreading Matthew's Eschatology

The Eschatological Discourse of chapters 24–25 has been among the most intensively read and most frequently misapplied sections of the Gospel, generating predictions and interpretive schemes that have consistently proven mistaken while continuing to attract readers convinced that the key to the discourse's meaning lies in identifying its predictions with contemporary events.

Matthew's Jesus carefully resists the calendar-setting his disciples' question invites. After describing tribulations and warning against false messiahs, he provides the interpretive key to the entire discourse: no one knows about that day or hour, not even the angels in heaven, nor the Son, but only the Father. This statement consistently resists misreadings that treat the discourse's vivid imagery as a coded prediction of datable events.

The Eschatological Discourse is not designed to give the community information about when the end will occur. It is designed to shape the community's posture in the period of waiting — to call it to the watchful, active, faithful engagement with present responsibilities that the uncertainty of timing requires. The three parables that conclude the discourse — the ten virgins, the talents, and the sheep and the goats — are all about how to live in the present rather than about when the future will arrive. Reading the discourse in light of these parables rather than in light of the vivid imagery of tribulation that precedes them produces a fundamentally different understanding of what the discourse is asking of its readers.

Misreading the Immanuel Theme

One further misreading concerns the Immanuel theme that brackets Matthew's entire narrative. The declaration in chapter 1 that the child will be called Immanuel, God with us, and the promise in chapter 28 that Jesus will be with his community always, to the very end of the age, frame the Gospel with the theme of divine presence. One common misreading spiritualizes this presence in a way that drains it of its concreteness — God with us becomes a feeling of divine accompaniment, an interior sense of spiritual support, rather than the actual presence of a specific person who has risen from the dead.

Matthew's Immanuel is not primarily a spiritual experience. It is a specific person, identified by name and genealogy and ministry and death and resurrection, who is present with his community in concrete ways that produce concrete effects. He is present when two or three gather in his name. He is present in the face of the vulnerable, the hungry, the stranger, the sick, and the imprisoned. He is present in the proclamation of the word and the administration of baptism. These are not metaphors for a spiritual sensation. They are descriptions of the modes of presence of a risen person who has promised to remain with his community through specific, historically identifiable means. Recovering this concreteness is essential to receiving what Matthew's framing of the entire Gospel is designed to give.

62

Chapter 7

What It Means for Modern Life

*"Therefore, everyone who hears these words of mine and puts them
into practice is like a wise man who built his house on the rock."*
— Matthew 7:24

Living Under the Reign of God

For modern readers who take Matthew seriously, the first and
most fundamental implication is the one the Gospel never stops
pressing: the kingdom of heaven has come near, and this changes
everything about how life is to be lived. Not everything about the
external circumstances of life — Matthew does not promise
wealth, security, or social approval to those who follow Jesus. But
everything about how those circumstances are engaged, what they
are for, and what gives them their ultimate meaning.

Living under the reign of God means, practically, that the
standards Matthew commends in the Sermon on the Mount are
not optional supplements to a life organized around other primary
goals. They describe the shape of life as it is meant to be lived
from within a genuine reorientation toward God. The person who
takes the Sermon seriously as more than moral advice will find it
reordering their priorities at precisely the points where the
surrounding culture — which tends to organize life around
achievement, accumulation, security, and approval — pushes in
the opposite direction.

The first and most foundational feature of life under God's
reign is simply this: it has a different center of gravity than life
organized under any of the other authority claims the surrounding
world makes. When Jesus asks in the Sermon on the Mount
whether people can serve two masters — whether they can be

fundamentally organized around God and around wealth simultaneously — the question is not hypothetical. It addresses the precise condition of people who are trying to live with genuine religious commitment within a world whose most powerful institutions are organized around different and competing centers.

This choosing is not a single act performed once and then settled. It is a practice that must be renewed continuously, because the competing centers exert their gravitational pull continuously. The formation that Matthew's five discourses describe is formation in the habits of orientation that allow a person to keep making this choice in the specific practical circumstances of daily life — to keep returning to the center rather than drifting away from it, to keep bringing actual decisions about money and relationships and power and status under the framework that the kingdom provides.

The Practical Reordering of Daily Life

The implications of living under the reign of God are both more specific and more demanding than most presentations of Christian discipleship tend to acknowledge. Matthew's Jesus does not speak in generalities about trusting God and being kind to others. He speaks with unusual precision about the specific dimensions of daily life where the values of the kingdom and the values of the surrounding culture come into direct and irresolvable conflict.

The teaching on wealth in the Sermon on the Mount is perhaps the most consistently avoided of these specific dimensions. You cannot serve God and wealth. Do not store up treasures on earth. Where your treasure is, there your heart will be also. These are specific claims about the relationship between a person's use of economic resources and the actual orientation of their interior life. Matthew's Jesus is not saying that wealth is inherently sinful. He is saying that the accumulation of wealth as an end in itself, as the primary project around which a life is

organized, is incompatible with the reorientation toward the
kingdom that genuine discipleship requires.

For communities living in societies shaped by consumer
capitalism — in which the accumulation of material goods and
financial security is actively promoted as the primary expression of
a successful life — this teaching creates a specific and demanding
challenge. It is not a challenge that can be met by the occasional
charitable donation or by giving a percentage of one's income to
religious and charitable causes while organizing the remainder of
one's financial life according to the logic of accumulation. It is a
challenge to the fundamental orientation of one's economic life —
to what money is for, to what financial security is supposed to
achieve, to the relationship between one's economic choices and
one's actual deepest commitments.

The teaching on status and social position is equally specific.
In chapter 23, Jesus describes those who love to be greeted with
respect in the marketplace, who want to be called rabbi and
teacher and father by others, who take the best seats at banquets.
These are not descriptions of people who are unusually vain or
whose character is especially defective. They are descriptions of
normal human behavior in social contexts shaped by honor and
status. Matthew's Jesus identifies this behavior as incompatible
with the character of the kingdom community: the greatest among
you will be your servant. This is not a reversal that leaves the
social hierarchy intact but simply inverts its values. It is a
description of a different kind of social organization altogether, in
which the measure of greatness is not position but service.

The Beatitudes as a Counter-Cultural Vision

The Beatitudes at the opening of the Sermon do not describe the
people whom contemporary culture celebrates. They describe the
poor in spirit, those who mourn, the meek, those who hunger for
righteousness, the merciful, the pure in heart, the peacemakers,

and those who are persecuted for righteousness. These are not the characteristics rewarded by a competitive economy or a culture of performance.

The Beatitudes are counter-cultural in their most fundamental structure, because they describe as blessed — as the recipients of the kingdom's goods — people who are in conditions of need, vulnerability, and marginality rather than conditions of achievement, security, and social standing. Every culture tends to organize its measures of value around achievement and success. The Beatitudes consistently subvert this tendency by insisting that the kingdom's measures of value are organized around a different axis entirely.

The poor in spirit are those who have come to recognize, with genuine honesty, that they have nothing to bring to God — that their spiritual resources are insufficient, that they are genuinely dependent on something they cannot produce for themselves. This is not an attractive condition in a culture that rewards confidence and projects of self-improvement. It is the condition that every serious engagement with the Sermon on the Mount, honestly pursued, eventually produces the recognition that what the Sermon asks for is beyond what self-improvement can supply. The first Beatitude thus functions as a kind of gateway into the entire Sermon: the person who has genuinely encountered poverty of spirit is positioned to receive what the Sermon offers in a way that the person who has not is not.

Those who mourn are those who are genuinely grieving — whether over their own failures and the failures of the world, over genuine losses, or over the distance between the world as it is and the world as the kingdom promises it will be. Contemporary culture is deeply uncomfortable with grief. The therapeutic imperative to process and move on, the cultural pressure to maintain a positive orientation toward life: all of these create pressure to minimize the time spent in grief and to treat its continuing presence as a problem to be solved. Matthew's second

Beatitude insists that those who mourn will be comforted — not that their grief will be eliminated but that the comfort the kingdom brings is real and specifically addressed to the condition of those who grieve.

The meek are those who lack the power or status to impose their will on the situations they inhabit. In a culture that celebrates assertiveness and self-advocacy, meekness is easily read as weakness or the failure to stand up for oneself. Matthew's third Beatitude insists that the meek will inherit the earth — a claim that seems to contradict every observable feature of how power actually operates in human societies. But the Beatitude is not describing how the present arrangement of power works. It is announcing the character of the kingdom's reversal of that arrangement.

Poverty of spirit, in the context of formation in the kingdom, is not an achievement but a discovery — the gradual recognition, through honest engagement with the Sermon and genuine discipleship, that the resources one has are not equal to the task one has been given. This recognition is not discouraging in the context of Matthew's Gospel because it is immediately accompanied by the announcement that the kingdom of heaven belongs to precisely those who have made this discovery.

Forgiveness as a Way of Life

No theme in Matthew's Gospel has more immediate relevance to modern life than forgiveness. Chapter 18's extended treatment — from the parable of the lost sheep through the community discipline process to the parable of the unforgiving servant — makes clear that forgiveness in Matthew is not merely an emotional response to being wronged. It is a practice, a discipline, a fundamental orientation of the community that bears the name of Christ.

The parable of the unforgiving servant makes the connection between forgiveness received and forgiveness extended inescapably clear. The servant who has been forgiven an enormous debt and then refuses to forgive a minor one has not simply failed to meet an ethical obligation. He has failed to allow what happened to him to actually change him. Modern readers who take this parable seriously will recognize how readily the patterns it describes appear in contemporary life — in families, in workplaces, in churches, in political communities — and how consistently the capacity to forgive remains one of the most difficult and most humanly necessary things Matthew calls its readers to.

Matthew's teaching on forgiveness does not conflict with the legitimate concern for accountability. The community discipline process that chapter 18 describes begins with honest confrontation — go and show them their fault — rather than with silent forgiveness that leaves the wrong unaddressed. Forgiveness in Matthew is not the silencing of legitimate grievance or the erasure of genuine harm in the interests of institutional peace.

What Matthew's forgiveness teaching adds to the concern for accountability is a recognition that the long-term maintenance of grievance as the organizing center of a community's identity produces destructive consequences independent of whether the grievance is just. Communities organized primarily around their grievances tend to become defined by those grievances in ways that crowd out the other things they are called to be and to do. Matthew's seventy-seven times does not mean that wrongs should not be addressed or that the same pattern of harm should be allowed to continue. It means that the orientation of the community toward those who have wronged it should not be governed primarily by the accounting of those wrongs but by the same abundance of grace the community itself has received.

The instruction to go directly to the person who has wronged you — just between the two of you — reflects a social wisdom that recognizes how quickly private grievances become public conflicts when shared with others before being addressed with the person concerned. This instruction is genuinely countercultural in the contemporary moment, where patterns of social media complaint, online exposure, and public shaming have become increasingly common forms of addressing perceived wrongs that consistently bypass the direct engagement Matthew prescribes. Direct confrontation requires a willingness to be honest about being hurt — a form of vulnerability that the surrounding culture tends to discourage. Matthew's instruction assumes that the goal is the restoration of the relationship, and that the difficulty of direct engagement is worth accepting in service of that goal.

Care for the Vulnerable as an Encounter with Christ

The parable of the sheep and the goats in chapter 25 offers one of the most searching formulations of social ethics in all of Scripture. The criterion of judgment is not doctrinal correctness or liturgical observance. It is the practical care extended to the hungry, the thirsty, the stranger, the poorly clothed, the sick, and the imprisoned. And the reason this care matters is not merely that it addresses human need — it is that in addressing the need of the vulnerable, those who do so are, without knowing it, encountering Christ himself.

This identification of Christ with the vulnerable has profound implications for how modern communities of faith understand their responsibilities. The care of the vulnerable is not a secondary concern to be addressed after the primary work of worship, teaching, and community building is complete. It is itself an encounter with the living Christ — a form of worship in action.

The identification of Christ with the vulnerable is not a metaphor. Matthew presents it as a fact about the present reality of Christ's presence in the world after his resurrection and before his return — a form of presence that extends into the places of greatest human vulnerability. Communities that have organized their life primarily around the formation of their existing members are challenged by Matthew 25 to ask whether they are encountering the Christ present in the vulnerable with the same seriousness as the Christ present in the word and the sacraments and the gathered assembly.

The six categories of vulnerability Matthew 25 identifies — the hungry, the thirsty, the stranger, the poorly clothed, the sick, and the imprisoned — are representative examples chosen to be concrete and specific rather than abstract and general. The stranger — the foreigner, the outsider, the one who does not belong — is in many contemporary contexts one of the most politically charged categories in the list. In societies where immigration and refugee policy have become flashpoints for intense political conflict, Matthew's identification of Christ with the stranger creates an immediate and unavoidable challenge. The teaching does not resolve complex policy questions about how societies should manage borders. But it insists with complete clarity that the stranger is a person in whom Christ is present and whose welcome or rejection is the welcome or rejection of Christ himself. Communities of faith cannot treat the stranger primarily as a political problem to be managed.

The imprisoned are perhaps the most easily overlooked category in contemporary Western societies, where incarceration has become so widespread that its human dimensions are easily obscured by its institutional scale. Matthew's identification of Christ with the imprisoned does not distinguish between those incarcerated justly and those who are not. It extends the identification to the whole category, and the visit it calls for is a form of presence that acknowledges the humanity of the imprisoned person rather than the category of their offense.

The Great Commission and the Shape of Mission

Matthew's final passage — the Great Commission — remains one of the most regularly cited and most regularly misunderstood texts in Christian life. Its call to make disciples of all nations has often been interpreted primarily as a mandate for geographical expansion. This dimension is genuinely present in the text, but Matthew's formulation is more comprehensive than a simple call to evangelism.

Making disciples in Matthew's sense involves baptizing and teaching — bringing people into the community and forming them in the way of life that Jesus has taught throughout the Gospel. The content of that teaching is not a brief summary of doctrinal essentials but the full scope of what Matthew has presented: the Beatitudes, the Sermon on the Mount, the community ethics of chapter 18, the great parables of the kingdom, the care for the vulnerable of chapter 25. The Great Commission is a commission to reproduce, in every nation, the kind of fully formed community that Matthew's entire Gospel has been describing.

The Great Commission has been one of the most energizing and, at times, one of the most problematic texts in the history of Christian mission. Its energizing force is evident: the conviction that the community of Jesus' followers has a responsibility to extend the knowledge of the gospel across every cultural and national boundary has motivated extraordinary commitments of life and resources across the centuries. Its problematic history is equally evident: the Great Commission has been used to justify forms of mission inseparable from colonialism, that required the erasure of indigenous cultures as the condition of Christian belonging, and that confused the imperialism of specific historical powers with the universal scope of the kingdom of heaven.

Reading the Great Commission in light of Matthew's Gospel as a whole provides the correction these problematic historical forms of mission need. The community Jesus is commissioning is the community shaped by the Sermon on the Mount's ethics of humility, nonretaliation, and care for the vulnerable — not the community that wields power in the manner of the Gentile rulers who lord it over their subjects, which Jesus explicitly contrasts with the pattern of the kingdom in chapter 20. The making of disciples that Jesus commissions is the making of people formed in the full content of his teaching and living it out in concrete communities shaped by the practices of the kingdom. This is not a commission that can be fulfilled by the announcement of doctrinal content alone, by the extraction of individuals from their communities into religious membership, or by the imposition of one culture's forms of Christian practice as the universal norm.

The Promise That Grounds the Commission

The Great Commission concludes with a promise at least as significant as the command it accompanies: I am with you always, to the very end of the age. This promise is not an afterthought or a pastoral encouragement added to soften the demanding character of the commission. It is the ground on which the commission rests — the reason the community can undertake a task of this scope without being paralyzed by the recognition that it far exceeds its own resources.

The promise of the abiding presence of Christ is the culmination of the Immanuel theme that Matthew announced at its very beginning. The child born of Mary will be called Immanuel — God with us. The Gospel that opened with this announcement closes with its fulfillment: I am with you always. The presence of God with his people, which was the fundamental promise of the covenant from its beginning, has found its definitive and permanent expression in the risen Christ who promises to remain with his community to the end of the age. This is not a general statement about divine providence. It is a specific promise about the concrete, personal, ongoing presence of the specific person who has been the subject of Matthew's entire narrative.

For communities undertaking the work of mission in the contemporary world — a world in many respects less hospitable to the claims of the gospel than the world of previous generations, where the cultural supports for Christian commitment have significantly eroded — this promise is the primary resource from which faithful engagement draws. The ground of the community's continuing engagement is not its confidence in the effectiveness of its methods or the adequacy of its resources. It is the promise of the one who has given it the task and who has promised to remain with it through every stage of its pursuit.

The Sermon's Demands in Contemporary Life

The practical implications of the Sermon on the Mount for contemporary life extend across every dimension of the experience of those who take it seriously. The teaching on anger and its relationship to murder addresses the inner life of the community at the level of the specific emotional responses that most frequently generate conflict and harm in daily relationships. The teaching on lust addresses the specifically sexual dimension of the interior life in a cultural context that has generated both heightened awareness of the harms produced by sexual exploitation and deep confusion about the character and purpose of human sexuality. The teaching on honesty and the inadequacy of oaths addresses the daily texture of speech in a cultural context where the performance of credibility has become a sophisticated art form.

Each of these teachings, taken seriously in the specific circumstances of contemporary life, produces the same kind of challenge: the challenge to allow the interior life to be genuinely addressed rather than simply the outer behavior to be managed more carefully. The person who addresses their anger seriously, not merely its outward expression, will find that this requires a different kind of engagement with their daily life than the management of behavior alone. The practices of prayer, of honest relationship, of willingness to be held accountable by others who are also committed to the same formation: these are the conditions under which the interior work the Sermon requires can actually happen.

Matthew's Gospel is not primarily a set of instructions for spiritual self-improvement. It is a portrait of a person and a community — Jesus and the community he forms — and an argument that the encounter with this person and participation in this community is the condition under which the life the Sermon describes becomes genuinely possible. The Sermon on the Mount is not achievable by effort directed at the Sermon's standards. It is achievable, gradually and imperfectly and always by grace, through the relationship with Jesus that Matthew's entire narrative describes and commends. This is what it means for the Sermon to be kingdom ethics rather than moral philosophy — it is the description of life in a kingdom that has a king, and the life it describes is possible because the king is present.

Chapter 8

Modern Reflection

"For where two or three gather in my name, there am I with them."
— Matthew 18:20

Matthew and the Question of Authentic Community

The previous chapter examined what Matthew's Gospel makes possible for modern readers — how its specific teachings on wealth, status, forgiveness, mission, and the care of the vulnerable can be applied as practical resources for daily life. This chapter is concerned with a different question: what Matthew does to the reader over time. Not the immediate application of a text to a specific situation, but the slower, less visible formation that happens when a person engages with the Gospel seriously and repeatedly across different seasons of life.

One of the most pressing questions facing modern culture is whether genuine community is possible in a world shaped by fragmentation, mobility, digital mediation, and performative identity. The longing for community is everywhere evident — in the appeal of social media, in the proliferation of interest groups and subcultures, in the persistent sense that the connections available in modern life do not fully satisfy the depth of human need for belonging. Matthew's Gospel does not address this question directly, but its vision of the community of disciples speaks to it with surprising relevance.

The community Matthew envisions is not a collection of individuals who happen to share certain beliefs. It is a community defined by specific practices — forgiveness, reconciliation, accountability, care for the vulnerable — and by the promise of a presence that transcends what any human gathering can produce on its own. The repeated emphasis on doing rather than merely professing, on interior transformation rather than outward performance, and on the care of the marginalized as a fundamental community practice all describe a form of life together that is counter to the tendencies of a consumer culture in which community is something to be found rather than built.

The longing for community in the contemporary moment has a specific shape that tells us something important about what has been lost and what is being sought. Geographic mobility means that many people live at significant distance from their families of origin and from the communities in which they were formed. The decline of institutional structures — churches, civic organizations, neighborhood associations — that previously provided ready-made frameworks for community has left many people without an obvious context for sustained relationship. Digital technologies have produced forms of connection that are often wide but rarely deep, providing the sensation of belonging without the substance. The community being sought is often imagined as a place that is found rather than built, that meets needs rather than makes demands, that provides belonging without the costs of genuine accountability. This is not a criticism of those who carry this longing — the longing is legitimate and the conditions that produced it are real. But it is a recognition that the community Matthew envisions may require a significant revision of the expectations with which the search for community begins.

The Distinctive Character of Matthew's Community

Matthew's community discourse in chapter 18 describes the community of disciples with unusual specificity, and the specificity itself is instructive. The community is defined primarily by shared practice — by the specific things its members do in relation to one another and to those outside it. The practices chapter 18 identifies are not optional features of community life that can be present or absent without affecting its fundamental character. They are constitutive: they are what makes the community the community.

The practice of seeking the one who has gone astray is embedded in the parable of the lost sheep. A community that does not pursue those who wander treats membership as fundamentally passive — something one has until one loses it, rather than something one is held in by the active care of the community. The parable insists on active pursuit rather than passive maintenance. Those who wander are sought, not simply mourned.

The practice of honest confrontation is perhaps the most uncomfortable in a cultural context that tends to value the avoidance of conflict above the pursuit of honesty. Go and show them their fault, just between the two of you. The instruction is precise: the person who has been wronged initiates the conversation, privately, with the goal of restoration rather than vindication. This process is in direct tension with the most common alternatives — avoidance, which allows conflicts to remain unaddressed until they become either explosive or permanently corrosive; gossip, which spreads the grievance to others before addressing the person concerned; and public exposure, which makes the conflict visible to a wide audience before any attempt has been made to resolve it privately. All of these alternatives are understandable responses to the discomfort of direct confrontation, but all tend to produce outcomes worse than what Matthew's process, difficult as it is, is designed to achieve.

The Failure of Digital Community

The emergence of digital platforms as the primary context for social connection has produced a specific and identifiable set of problems for community that Matthew's vision speaks to with striking directness. The fundamental problem with digital community is that it is conducted at a level of abstraction from the full reality of persons that genuine community requires. When community happens through a screen, participants are present to each other in a carefully curated and significantly reduced form. The physical presence of another person — their bodily reality, their facial expressions, their tone of voice — is replaced by text, images, and managed presentations of identity. The community that forms under these conditions is real in some senses, but it is systematically thinner than genuine community, because the persons who constitute it are present to each other in a reduced form.

Matthew's community is constituted by the presence of Christ among those who gather in his name — a presence specifically located in the bodily gathering of the community. Where two or three gather in my name, there am I with them. The gathering is not merely incidental to the community's constitution. It is essential to it. This is why Matthew's community practices — the pursuit of the one who has wandered, the face-to-face confrontation of conflict, the shared meal, communal decision-making — are all practices of bodily presence rather than digital connection. The work of genuine community cannot be fully realized through digital means, however useful digital tools might be for certain aspects of community life.

The Beatitudes and Contemporary Culture

The eight Beatitudes read, in the context of contemporary culture, as a nearly comprehensive inversion of the values that ambient society rewards. Poverty of spirit runs counter to the cultural premium on self-sufficiency and confidence. Meekness runs counter to assertiveness. Mourning is something to be managed and overcome rather than inhabited. And yet the enduring power of these words is hard to deny. They return to readers generation after generation with a quality that resists easy dismissal — a recognition that what they describe, however countercultural, touches something real.

The power of the Beatitudes in the contemporary moment is most clearly visible when read against the specific forms that competing cultural values take in daily experience. The premium on self-sufficiency manifests in constant pressure to project capability and competence in professional contexts, to perform adequacy in social contexts, to manage the impression one creates in ways that consistently screen out the vulnerability that poverty of spirit represents. The social media economy has amplified these pressures enormously, creating platforms in which the performance of success, happiness, and social approval is both expected and systematically rewarded.

Against this background, the first Beatitude functions not merely as a description of a blessed condition but as a diagnosis of what the prevailing economy of self-presentation costs those who participate in it. The cost is the disconnection between the performed self and the actual self that sustained performance gradually deepens. The person who performs self-sufficiency long enough finds they have lost touch with the reality of their own need — the poverty of spirit that is in fact their condition has been covered over by so many layers of performed adequacy that they can no longer access it honestly.

The Beatitude about mourning deserves particular attention in a cultural context that has generated both unprecedented awareness of the world's suffering through global media and an extraordinary range of mechanisms for managing the response to that awareness. The structures of contemporary life provide abundant means for not genuinely feeling the suffering of others — for consuming information about it in a form that generates concern without grief, awareness without engagement. Matthew's second Beatitude blesses those who allow themselves to grieve the specific, concrete sufferings of specific, concrete people rather than managing those sufferings at the level of abstract concern.

Anxiety and the Sermon on the Mount

Chapter 6 of Matthew contains some of the most directly pastoral material in the New Testament — the teaching on anxiety that follows the Lord's Prayer. Do not worry about your life, what you will eat or drink; or about your body, what you will wear. This is not naive optimism. It is a sustained argument about where genuine security comes from and what anxiety actually reveals about the state of trust in a person's life.

In an era of documented anxiety epidemic — particularly among younger generations — this passage has acquired peculiar relevance. Matthew does not counsel indifference to practical concerns about food, clothing, health, and relationships. It redirects attention: seek first the kingdom of God and his righteousness, and all these things will be given to you as well. The argument is not that material needs do not matter but that they are not the right organizing center of a life. When they become the organizing center, the anxiety they generate is a symptom of misplaced trust.

The anxiety epidemic of the contemporary moment is broadly a condition in which people experience the conditions of their lives — their relationships, their health, their social standing, their performance at work — as sources of existential threat that must be continuously managed. The management consumes enormous energy and produces, paradoxically, more anxiety rather than less, because the attempt to control what cannot ultimately be controlled generates an escalating cycle of effort and insufficient result. Matthew's response to this cycle is not to offer better management techniques. It is to identify the cycle itself as a symptom of the wrong organizing center and to offer a different one.

Forgiveness in an Age of Grievance

There may be no theme in Matthew more directly countercultural in the contemporary moment than forgiveness. The political and cultural climate of the early twenty-first century has produced a remarkable proliferation of grievance — the documentation and prosecution of wrongs done, the demand for accountability and reparation. These concerns are not without legitimate grounding. Accountability matters; justice matters. Matthew does not deny any of this.

But Matthew's teaching on forgiveness insists that the accumulation of grievance is not a sustainable foundation for community life or personal integrity. The person who cannot forgive is not simply failing to meet a generous standard. They are, in Matthew's vision, imprisoning themselves in a relationship with their offender that perpetuates damage rather than ending it.

The grievance culture that has developed in Western societies over recent decades is not simply the product of self-indulgence. It is the product of genuine historical wrongs that were long denied and genuine patterns of abuse and exploitation that were long covered. The exposure of these wrongs represents a genuine advance in moral clarity, and Matthew's teaching on forgiveness does not require the reversal of that advance. What it does require is a recognition that the demand for acknowledgment, justice, and repair — however legitimate — cannot be the organizing center of a community's life without producing consequences that are destructive to the community as well as to the offender. The community organized primarily around its grievances tends to become increasingly unable to engage with those outside it who do not share its particular history of wrong, and increasingly unable to imagine a future that is not primarily the prosecution of the past.

The parable of the unforgiving servant illuminates this dynamic with unusual precision. The servant who has been released from an enormous debt goes out immediately and begins to choke a fellow servant over a much smaller debt. The contrast is not meant to suggest that the smaller debt is not real or that the fellow servant is not genuinely in the wrong. It is meant to reveal the incoherence of a person who has genuinely received grace and allowed that grace to produce no change in how they relate to others who have wronged them. Matthew's seventy-seven times is the response to this incoherence — an insistence that the orientation of the community toward those who have wronged it must be shaped by the abundance of grace it has received rather than by the logic of debt and repayment that governs the unformed version of human community.

Authority and Leadership

Matthew's Gospel contains some of the most searching reflections on authority and leadership in the entire New Testament. The defining passage appears in chapter 20, in the exchange that follows James and John's request for seats of honor. Jesus' response draws a precise contrast between two fundamentally different models of authority. The model of the Gentile rulers is one in which authority expresses itself through the exercise of power over others, through the maintenance of hierarchical distance, and through the extraction of service from those below. This is the model that every human institutional structure tends to default toward, because it most efficiently serves the interests of those who hold authority. The model Jesus both describes and embodies is one in which authority expresses itself through service to others, through the willingness to take the lowest position rather than the highest, and through the offering of one's own life for the benefit of those over whom authority is theoretically held.

The implications for the exercise of authority in communities of faith are both clear and demanding. Leadership in the community of the kingdom is not the management of an institution in the interests of its continued existence. It is not the cultivation of a personal following or the building of a reputation for religious insight. It is the specific and costly practice of placing the needs and formation of others above the comfort and advancement of oneself.

The Promise That Grounds Community Life

The promise of Matthew 28 — I am with you always, to the very end of the age — is the last word of Matthew's Gospel, and its placement at the conclusion of the entire narrative is deliberate. The Immanuel announcement at the beginning — God with us — finds its fulfillment and confirmation in this final declaration.

For communities navigating the specific challenges of a cultural context significantly less hospitable to the claims of the gospel than the context of previous generations, this promise is the primary resource from which faithful engagement draws. The community that takes seriously its calling to embody the kingdom in specific, costly, concrete ways in the world will encounter resistance, misunderstanding, and the simple difficulty of the task. The ground of its continuing engagement is not its own enthusiasm or confidence in the effectiveness of its methods. It is the promise of the one who has given it the task and who has promised to remain with it through every stage of its pursuit.

The modes of Christ's presence in the contemporary community are the modes Matthew's Gospel identifies throughout its narrative: in the gathered assembly, in the word proclaimed and taught, in the sacramental breaking of bread, in the face of the vulnerable, and in the disciplines of prayer, forgiveness, and mutual accountability that the community discourse describes as the constitutive practices of kingdom community. The community that attends carefully to these modes of presence — that gathers with genuine expectation, teaches with genuine fidelity, shares the bread with genuine recognition, serves the vulnerable with genuine care, and practices forgiveness with genuine commitment — is the community that is genuinely experiencing the promise with which Matthew's Gospel ends, and that will find in that experience the resources it needs to continue its life in the world with the faithfulness the Gospel commends.

Chapter 9

Reflection Questions

"Let the one who has ears, let them hear."
— Matthew 13:9

Questions for Engagement with Matthew's Gospel

Matthew's Gospel is designed not to be read passively but to be engaged with actively — tested against experience, brought into conversation with the realities of daily life, and returned to repeatedly with the expectation that it will continue to yield insight. The following questions are offered as starting points for that kind of sustained engagement, whether in personal study, group discussion, or ongoing reflection.

These questions are not designed to have definitive answers. Matthew's Gospel has sustained serious engagement for nearly two thousand years precisely because its depth does not exhaust itself on first encounter. The questions that follow are invitations to the kind of sustained, honest, repeatedly renewed engagement that the Gospel itself commends. They are designed to be returned to in different seasons of life and different stages of understanding, with the expectation that what they yield will change as the reader changes and as the circumstances of their community and their world change around them.

On the Kingdom of Heaven

Matthew's Jesus announces that the kingdom of heaven has come near. What difference does it make whether this announcement is received as genuinely true versus merely as an inspiring metaphor? Where in your own experience do you most clearly see — or most clearly feel the absence of — the reality that Matthew calls the kingdom of heaven?

Before the more specific questions about the kingdom's character and demands can be engaged honestly, the foundational question must be faced: do you believe the kingdom of heaven has actually arrived, in the specific form that Matthew's Gospel claims it has? Not in principle, not as a general religious conviction that God's sovereignty over creation is in some sense operative — but specifically, in the person and ministry and death and resurrection of Jesus of Nazareth. The answer to this question determines the framework within which all other questions about the kingdom are asked. If the kingdom has genuinely arrived, then the ethics of the Sermon on the Mount are not an impossible ideal but a description of the life that is genuinely possible for those who have received the kingdom's gift. If the kingdom has genuinely arrived, then care for the vulnerable is not a humanitarian obligation but an encounter with the living Christ. The difference between receiving the kingdom announcement as genuinely true and receiving it as an inspiring metaphor is not primarily a matter of theological precision. It is a practical difference that shapes the entire character of the life that flows from it.

Consider the parables of chapter thirteen and the specific images they offer of the kingdom's character in the present moment. Which of the four kinds of soil most honestly describes your own reception of the kingdom at this point in your life? Not which kind you would most like to be, but which most accurately describes the condition of your actual engagement with the kingdom's claims now. Is the word being received and bearing fruit, or is it being choked by competing concerns, or is it growing in shallow soil that produces initial enthusiasm without the depth that sustains it through difficulty?

The parable of the weeds growing alongside the wheat addresses the specific temptation of those who have received the kingdom to want to purify the community by removing those who seem to be false disciples. The sorting will happen at the harvest, not before. What does this mean for how you relate to those in your community whose commitment to the kingdom seems less genuine than yours? The parable is addressed to the community's impulse toward premature purification, but it is also implicitly addressed to the individual's tendency to locate the weed in others rather than acknowledging the mixture that exists within oneself.

The parables of the hidden treasure and the pearl of great price ask the most searching question about the kingdom's place in your actual life: is it the organizing center around which everything else is arranged, or is it one significant concern among several that compete for your primary loyalty? Is there an area of your life that you are holding back from the reorganization the kingdom's arrival calls for? What is it, and what does holding it back cost you in terms of the kind of life Matthew's Gospel describes as possible for those who receive the kingdom fully?

On the Sermon on the Mount

The Beatitudes describe eight conditions that the kingdom addresses and reverses. Which of the eight is most difficult to receive as genuinely good news in your own experience? The antitheses of Matthew 5 trace familiar commandments back to their interior roots — from murder to anger, from adultery to lust, from broken oaths to the condition of the heart that makes them necessary. What interior conditions in your own life do the commands of the Sermon actually address?

The Beatitudes do not describe eight separate categories of person but eight dimensions of the human condition that the kingdom addresses. The category that is most difficult to receive as genuinely good news is usually the most revealing. If poverty of spirit is difficult to receive, the difficulty usually reveals something about the degree to which self-sufficiency has become a fundamental value in one's self-understanding. If mourning is difficult to receive as a blessed condition, the difficulty usually reveals something about the degree to which the management of grief rather than its genuine engagement has become the default response to loss.

The diagnostic function of the Beatitudes — their capacity to reveal the actual conditions of the interior life when engaged honestly rather than appreciated from a distance — is one of the most practically valuable things they offer. The question is not which Beatitude describes your aspiration but which one most honestly names your actual condition. Where is the genuine condition in your life that corresponds to one of these eight descriptions, and what would it mean to allow the Beatitude that addresses it to speak to your actual situation rather than to your idealized one?

The antitheses of chapter 5 are designed to do a specific kind of work in the person who engages them honestly: they move the locus of moral examination from the level of behavior, where it is relatively comfortable, to the level of the interior life, where it is much less so. The question the antitheses are asking is not: have you committed murder, adultery, broken an oath? It is: what is the condition of your interior life at the level from which these behaviors grow? What do you do with anger before it reaches the level of expression that anyone else can observe? What is the actual quality of your attention to other people — are they persons to you or are they objects of various kinds of use?

The teaching on prayer in chapter 6 invites honest examination of actual prayer practice. How often do you actually pray, and what do you pray about? Does your prayer reflect the structure of the Lord's Prayer — oriented toward God, toward the kingdom, toward dependence and forgiveness and deliverance — or does it primarily reflect the concerns that organize your daily life, offered to God as a set of needs to be addressed? The Lord's Prayer is not a formula to be recited but a framework that shapes the orientation of the one who prays.

The teaching on anxiety at the end of chapter 6 invites the most personally direct examination: what are you anxious about, honestly, and what does that anxiety reveal about the organizing center of your life? Not what you are theoretically anxious about in abstract categories, but what specifically, concretely, keeps you awake at night or generates the kind of low-level chronic unease that is the contemporary form of the worry Matthew addresses. The question behind the anxiety is always: what am I organizing my life around that would be threatened if this went wrong?

The parable of the wise and foolish builders asks the final and most practical question: where is the gap between hearing and doing in your life with Matthew's Sermon? Not where are you doing it adequately, but where is the gap? Where is the area in which you hear the Sermon, recognize its claim, feel its force, and still do not put it into practice? What prevents the hearing from becoming doing in that area, and what would need to change for the gap to be closed?

On Discipleship and the Disciples

Matthew's disciples are people who genuinely follow and regularly fail. Where do you most recognize your own discipleship in their portrait — in their responsiveness or in their confusion and failure? Chapter 18 describes a community shaped by forgiveness, accountability, and care for the vulnerable. What specific practices would need to change in a community you belong to in order for it to look more like the community Matthew envisions?

The disciples' portrait in Matthew is valuable precisely because it refuses idealization. Peter, who confesses Jesus as the Messiah, and then, within a few moments, is rebuked as Satan. The disciples who witness the Transfiguration and then fail immediately afterward to heal a child in need. The disciples who scatter when Jesus is arrested, leaving him entirely alone. These are not stories about people who are fundamentally unlike those who follow Jesus in every subsequent generation. They are stories about the characteristic failure mode of genuine discipleship — the gap between what the disciple genuinely believes and genuinely intends and what they actually do when the conditions become genuinely testing.

Where in your own experience of discipleship is the gap between intention and action most consistent? The person who regularly resolves to pray and regularly fails to pray. The person who knows what genuine forgiveness requires and who consistently stops short of it. The person who is committed in principle to the care of the vulnerable and who consistently finds that other commitments have taken priority. These patterns of consistent shortfall are not evidence that genuine discipleship is absent. They are evidence that genuine discipleship is present but incomplete — that the formation that genuine following of Jesus requires is still in process.

The promise that the risen Christ makes at the end of Matthew — I am with you always, to the very end of the age — is not simply a reassurance about divine benevolence. It is a specific promise about the ongoing presence of the specific person whose story Matthew has told. How does this promise function in your actual experience of discipleship? Is it a conviction that shapes your daily engagement with the responsibilities you carry, or is it a theological affirmation that you hold without it having much practical bearing on how you actually operate?

The community discourse of chapter 18 is the most practically specific of Matthew's five discourses. Consider the community or communities to which you belong and ask honestly which of the practices it describes are present in recognizable form and which are absent. Is there a practice of pursuing those who wander rather than simply accepting their departure? Is there a practice of direct, honest confrontation of conflict rather than avoidance or gossip? Is there a practice of forgiveness that is practiced repeatedly rather than offered once and then exhausted?

The gap between the community that chapter 18 describes and the communities that most people inhabit in practice is usually significant, and acknowledging that gap honestly is the beginning of the work of closing it.

On Judgment and Accountability

The parable of the sheep and the goats presents care for the vulnerable as an encounter with Christ himself. What would it mean for a local church community to organize its common life around this identification? Matthew's eschatological parables consistently call for readiness rather than anxiety. What does it look like to live with genuine attentiveness to the present moment without allowing concern for the future to displace present faithfulness?

The parable of the sheep and the goats is among the most morally unsettling passages in the entire Gospel, and its unsettling quality is proportional to how honestly it is received. The righteous in the parable are not people who knew they were serving Christ in the vulnerable. They are people who were astonished to discover that they had been — people whose care for the hungry, thirsty, stranger, sick, and imprisoned was simply the expression of genuine concern for those in need. This detail is theologically significant because it means that the criterion the parable presents cannot be gamed — cannot be met by adopting the theological conviction that Christ is present in the vulnerable and then using that conviction as the motivation for calculated service.

What is your actual practice of engagement with the hungry, the thirsty, the stranger, the sick, and the imprisoned — not as an occasional exercise of charitable generosity, but as a regular feature of your community's life? The parable does not ask about grand charitable programs or impressive institutional responses to social need. It asks about the specific, concrete, personal response to the specific, concrete, personally encountered need of the person in front of you. What does that response look like in practice, and where is it most consistently absent from your community's life?

The parable of the ten virgins asks a question that is less comfortable than it might initially appear: are you genuinely prepared for the extended waiting that faithful discipleship requires, or is your readiness a superficial preparedness that cannot sustain itself through the period of apparent delay? The foolish virgins are not indifferent to the bridegroom's coming — they have taken their lamps and gone out to meet him. Their failure is not one of fundamental commitment but of practical preparation for the specific form that waiting takes. What in your own life corresponds to the extra oil that the wise virgins bring — the resources of prayer, of formed relationship, of sustained practice, of genuine community that make it possible to sustain faithfulness through periods when the kingdom's fullness is not immediately visible?

The parable of the talents raises the specific question of what you are doing with what has been entrusted to you. The talents represent not merely money but the full range of gifts, capacities, relationships, opportunities, and resources that have been entrusted to a specific person in the specific circumstances of their specific life. Where are you investing rather than burying what you have been given? The third servant's fear — his assessment of the master as harsh and demanding — is exposed as self-serving rather than accurate. Where in your own life does fear of failure or fear of risk lead you to bury what you have been given rather than put it to use?

On the Great Commission and Mission

The Great Commission at the end of Matthew — all authority has been given to me, therefore go and make disciples of all nations, baptizing and teaching — is the most explicit statement of the community's ongoing responsibility in Matthew's Gospel. What does it mean for you, specifically, in your specific situation, to participate in the making of disciples? Not the church's general responsibility to engage in mission, but your specific, concrete, particular participation in that responsibility given the specific gifts, relationships, contexts, and opportunities that characterize your actual life.

The teaching and baptizing that Matthew's commission pairs with going are not incidental to the commission but constitutive of it. What is actually being taught in the communities that bear Matthew's commission? Is it the full scope of what Matthew has presented — the Beatitudes, the Sermon on the Mount, the community ethics of chapter 18, the parables of the kingdom, the care for the vulnerable of chapter 25 — or is it a selective version of Matthew that emphasizes the more comfortable dimensions while minimizing the more demanding ones? The commission is not to reproduce comfortable community in every nation but to reproduce the fully formed kind of community that Matthew's Gospel describes.

Where are the specific boundaries — ethnic, economic, social, cultural — that the kingdom's universal scope calls your community to cross, and what is the actual quality of your engagement with people on the other side of those boundaries? The scope of the Great Commission is genuinely universal, and Matthew's Gospel has been moving toward this universality since the Magi of chapter 2. But universality in principle is not participation in practice, and the question of how a community's sense of universal responsibility connects to the specific forms of engagement that are available to it is one that requires practical wisdom rather than simply theological conviction.

The promise that grounds the commission — I am with you always — invites a question about how this promise is actually experienced in the practice of mission. Is the presence of Christ a living resource that the community engaged in mission actually draws on, that shapes the confidence and patience and resilience with which it pursues its work? Or is it a theological affirmation that is held abstractly without much bearing on the day-to-day experience of the work?

On the Passion and Resurrection

The Gethsemane account invites a specific kind of honest reflection on the experience of genuine wrestling with what God seems to be asking. Have you had experiences of genuine Gethsemane — experiences in which you knew what faithfulness required and found yourself genuinely resistant to it, in which you asked repeatedly whether the cup could be removed, and in which submission to the Father's will was an act of costly trust rather than serene acceptance? What did those experiences reveal about the nature of genuine obedience as Matthew presents it?

The account of Peter's denial is one of the most searching passages in the Gospel precisely because Peter's failure is not the failure of someone who never believed or who was never genuinely committed. It is the failure of someone whose commitment was genuine but whose courage, in the specific conditions of threat that the night of the arrest created, proved insufficient to sustain what he genuinely held. What conditions in your own life are most likely to produce the kind of failure that Peter's denial represents — the gap between what you genuinely believe and what you are able to sustain in practice when the cost of sustaining it becomes acute?

The resurrection narrative in chapter 28 is brief but theologically rich, and its brevity is itself instructive. Matthew does not provide a detailed phenomenological account of what the resurrection was like. He describes the event in terms of its effects and implications: the stone rolled back, the angel's announcement, the women's astonishment and joy, the disciples' worship and doubt on the mountain, and the commission that the risen Christ gives. What does the resurrection mean for the community's ongoing life? It is not primarily an experience to be described but a reality that reorganizes everything — establishing the authority of the one who commissions and the confidence of the community that is sent.

Questions for Continued Engagement

These questions are a beginning rather than an ending. Matthew's Gospel is designed to generate more questions the more carefully it is engaged — not because it is unclear but because it is deep, and depth generates questions that shallower engagement does not reach. The reader who returns to Matthew in six months or a year will find that the questions have changed, not because the Gospel has changed but because the reader has, and because new circumstances have made different dimensions of the Gospel newly relevant and newly pressing.

The most important thing about these questions is not that they be answered but that they be taken seriously. The taking seriously is itself a form of engagement with the Gospel that the Gospel commends. The person who asks honestly, who does not settle for easy answers, who continues to bring the questions back to the text and to the community and to the experience of life lived in light of what the text claims: this person is practicing the kind of engagement that Matthew describes as building on rock rather than sand. The house built on rock is not the house of those who have answered all the questions but the house of those who have heard and who keep putting into practice what they hear.

Matthew's Gospel will keep giving back more as its readers keep bringing more to it. The conversation that Matthew's Jesus initiates in the first century continues into every subsequent century with the same invitation and the same expectation: come and learn, hear and do, follow and be formed. That invitation remains open. These questions are one way of accepting it.

Chapter 10

Five Lessons

"Therefore, go and make disciples of all nations, baptizing them in the name of the Father and of the Son and of the Holy Spirit, and teaching them to obey everything I have commanded you."
— Matthew 28:19–20

Five Lessons from Matthew's Gospel

Matthew's Gospel has been shaping communities of faith for nearly two thousand years, and its capacity to do so has not diminished. The five lessons that follow are not five separate topics but five dimensions of a single underlying reality — five angles from which Matthew approaches the central claim that the kingdom of heaven has arrived in Jesus and that this arrival changes everything about how human life is to be lived. They are not a summary of Matthew's content so much as a distillation of the most persistent and most demanding things it asks of those who receive it.

Lesson One: The Kingdom Is Present and Demands a Response

Matthew's Gospel begins and ends with the announcement that something decisive has happened. The kingdom of heaven has come near. All authority in heaven and on earth has been given. These are not invitations to intellectual consideration but declarations that call for a response. Matthew's consistent concern is not whether its readers find the kingdom interesting or theologically plausible but whether they actually live in light of its arrival.

The announcement that the kingdom has come near is the first thing Jesus says in public in Matthew's Gospel, and its placement is deliberate. Everything which follows is to be understood within this frame: something has arrived, something decisive is happening, and the appropriate response is not observation but repentance — the turning of the whole self toward the reality that has arrived. The word translated repentance carries more weight than the English word typically suggests. It is not merely remorse for past failures or religious regret. It is a fundamental reorientation of the mind and will and desire toward the kingdom — a turning away from whatever has been functioning as the organizing center of one's life and a turning toward the one who announces and embodies the kingdom.

The urgency of this announcement is maintained throughout the Gospel through a series of literary and theological devices that consistently press the reader toward response. The call narratives press for immediate response with no provision for deliberation. The parables of the kingdom press for honest self-examination about the condition of one's reception. The eschatological parables press for watchful readiness rather than the comfortable assumption that there is always more time. And the Great Commission, which brings the narrative to its conclusion, presses the claim that all authority has been given to the one who sends the community on its mission — a claim that either commands the community's total allegiance or requires an account of why it does not.

The call to response in Matthew is not a call to a particular set of behaviors, though it has behavioral implications. It is a call to a particular orientation of the self — to the reorganization of one's life around a new center of gravity that displaces every other organizing principle that previously held that position. This is why the response Matthew consistently commends is characterized by the same totality that the disciples display in the call narratives: they leave everything and follow. This does not mean that every person who receives the kingdom's announcement must literally abandon their occupation and family. It means that the reorganization of life around Jesus as the center is genuinely total — that nothing is exempt from being reshaped by the kingdom's arrival, that no area of life is maintained as a private domain insulated from the claims the kingdom makes.

The parables of chapter 13 press the call to response from a different angle. The parable of the sower is not primarily a description of why some people receive the kingdom and others do not. It is an invitation to honest self-examination about which kind of soil one actually is — about the specific conditions that prevent the word from taking root in one's own life. The parables of the hidden treasure and the pearl of great price describe the reorganization of priorities that genuine discovery of the kingdom requires in terms that are both concrete and demanding: selling everything, not merely some things. The eschatological parables of chapter 25 return to the call for response with an urgency shaped by the specific problem of extended waiting. The ten virgins are all going out to meet the bridegroom — the division between them is not between those who are waiting and those who have given up, but between those who are prepared for waiting that turns out to be longer than expected and those who are not.

Lesson Two: Righteousness Is an Interior Matter

One of Matthew's most consistent and most searching lessons is that genuine righteousness — the quality of life the kingdom requires — cannot be produced by outward compliance alone. The scribes and Pharisees, in Matthew's portrait, are not indifferent to righteousness. They are intensely committed to it, and their commitment is visible, measurable, and publicly recognized. What they lack, in Jesus' analysis, is the interior transformation that would make their outward practice an authentic expression of the character it is meant to reflect.

For modern readers, this lesson is at least as uncomfortable as it was for first-century religious professionals. We live in a culture saturated with performance — with the careful management of public image, the strategic display of virtue, and the accumulation of credentials that signal the right commitments. Matthew's Gospel insists that none of this produces what it appears to produce. The test of genuine righteousness, in Matthew's vision, is not what is visible to others, but what is happening at the level of the interior life.

The Pharisees' failure in Matthew is not the failure of bad people pretending to be good. It is the failure of genuinely serious people who have invested enormous effort in the cultivation of visible religious excellence and who have, through that very investment, developed a subtle but devastating capacity to confuse the performance of righteousness with its possession. This confusion is not unique to the Pharisees. It is the characteristic failure of religious communities in every era, including communities that know about the Pharisees and are alert to the danger of repeating their mistake. The alertness to the danger does not immunize one against it; it can in fact become another form of the same performance — the careful maintenance of a reputation for not being Pharisaical that is itself a form of the same management of religious image that Matthew identifies as the problem.

The culture of performance that characterizes contemporary life is more pervasive than the performance that Matthew's Jesus identifies in the scribes and Pharisees. Contemporary performance is not confined to religious practice but extends across every dimension of social life: the management of one's professional reputation, the cultivation of one's social media presence, the careful presentation of one's parenting and relationships and moral commitments in ways that generate the approval of the communities whose judgment matters. Matthew's second lesson is that these performances are not producing what they appear to produce — because performance substitutes for the interior reality that genuine righteousness requires rather than expressing it. The person who performs generosity without possessing it has not become generous. The person who performs forgiveness without having actually released the grievance has not forgiven.

The Sermon on the Mount's description of interior transformation is specific in ways that are practically useful. The transformation of anger involves more than the management of angry impulses through techniques of emotional regulation. It involves the cultivation of a different relationship to the people who provoke anger — the genuine willingness to see them as persons rather than as obstacles or threats. The transformation of honesty involves more than the avoidance of explicit lies. It involves the cultivation of an interior integrity in which the gap between what one presents to others and what one knows to be true about oneself is genuinely closed, or at least consistently acknowledged and engaged rather than papered over with the convenient self-deceptions that make social life easier. These transformations are not achieved through willpower directed at behavioral management. They are achieved through the sustained relationship with Jesus that Matthew's entire narrative commends and through the community practices that Matthew's community discourse describes.

Lesson Three: The Vulnerable Are the Measure of the Kingdom

Throughout Matthew's Gospel, the treatment of the vulnerable — the sick, the outcast, the poor, the marginalized, the child — functions as an index of genuine participation in the kingdom of heaven. Jesus moves consistently toward those whom society has placed at the margins. His healings are not random demonstrations of power but responses to specific human need. His table fellowship with tax collectors and sinners is a concrete enactment of the kingdom's inclusive character.

The parable of the sheep and the goats brings this pattern to its most explicit theological statement: the criterion of judgment is the care extended to the most vulnerable, and the identification of Christ with those who are in need means that the encounter with the vulnerable is an encounter with him. The measure of a community's genuine participation in the kingdom is not the quality of its worship or the sophistication of its theology but its care for the hungry, the sick, and the stranger.

This pattern is established long before the parable of the sheep and the goats makes it theologically explicit. The healing ministry of chapters 8 and 9 moves systematically through encounters with people at the margins: a leper whose skin condition has placed him outside the social body, a Gentile soldier whose ethnicity places him outside the covenant community, a woman whose hemorrhage has rendered her ritually impure, a girl who is dead, two blind men who have nothing to recommend them except their need and their persistent faith. In each case, the margin is crossed rather than maintained. When the Baptist's disciples ask whether Jesus is the expected one, the evidence he offers is precisely this list of boundary-crossing activities: the blind see, the lame walk, the lepers are cleansed, the deaf hear, the dead are raised, the poor have good news proclaimed to them. This is the evidence that the kingdom has arrived — not the institutional endorsement of those who carry religious authority, but the specific reversal of the conditions that place specific people at the margins of the human community.

One of the most theologically concentrated moments in the community discourse comes when Jesus calls a little child to stand among the disciples and says: whoever takes the lowly position of this child is the greatest in the kingdom of heaven. The child in the ancient Mediterranean world was a social nobody — a person with no status, no rights, entirely dependent on the protection of adults and entirely without the capacity to contribute to the community's economy. To welcome a child was to welcome someone who could not reciprocate, who offered nothing in return. The one who extends care and welcome to someone who has nothing to offer in return is the one who is greatest in the kingdom's terms. And the one who humbles themselves to the position of the child — who accepts the condition of dependence, of receiving rather than achieving — has entered the kingdom in the form it actually takes.

The implications for the boundaries of contemporary communities of faith are significant and consistently uncomfortable. The community that maintains its identity primarily through the management of its boundaries — through careful distinction between who belongs and who does not — is operating according to a logic that Matthew's Jesus consistently challenges. The community that maintains its identity primarily through the extension of welcome — through the consistent movement toward those who need what the kingdom offers — is operating according to the logic that Matthew's Jesus consistently embodies and commends.

Lesson Four: Forgiveness Is the Oxygen of Community

Matthew's community discourse returns insistently to forgiveness because Matthew understands that the capacity to forgive is not optional for the kind of community the kingdom requires. A community that cannot forgive will eventually become defined by its grievances — organized around the documentation of wrongs done and the perpetuation of the divisions they created. The community Matthew envisions practices forgiveness as a discipline, not because wrongs do not matter, but because the maintenance of grievance destroys what it is supposed to protect.

The oxygen metaphor captures both the essential character of forgiveness for community life and the way its absence is experienced. A community that cannot forgive does not simply fail to practice a virtue it otherwise possesses. It begins to suffocate — to find the atmosphere of its common life increasingly toxic, organized around the management of past injuries rather than the pursuit of its shared vocation, increasingly unable to engage with the present because the past has claimed too much of its energy and attention.

The parable of the unforgiving servant is carefully constructed to illuminate the specific logic of unforgiveness. The contrast between the two debts — ten thousand talents and a hundred denarii — is so extreme as to be almost comic, but the comedy serves a serious purpose: it exposes the absurdity of the servant's behavior by making the disproportion between what he has received and what he refuses to extend too large to explain by anything other than the failure of grace to do its proper work. The servant has not become a monster. He has simply failed to be formed by what happened to him.

Matthew's community discourse provides the specific structures that support forgiveness without naively pretending that wrongs should go unaddressed or that genuine accountability is incompatible with genuine grace. The process of chapter 18 — go privately, bring witnesses, bring it before the community — takes wrong seriously enough to address it directly while maintaining the goal of restoration as the primary aim at every stage. The seventy-seven times formula establishes the fundamental orientation of forgiveness within this structured process. It is not a limit on how many times forgiveness can be extended. It is a refusal of the whole logic of counting, which is itself a form of the grievance-maintenance that forgiveness is designed to displace. The community that is counting how many times it has forgiven a particular person is still organized around the grievance. The community that has stopped counting — that has adopted the seventy-seven times orientation as the framework within which it engages all conflict — has begun to be formed in the way that Matthew commends.

The ground of forgiveness in Matthew is not human virtue but divine grace — not the extraordinary generosity of unusually forgiving people but the experience of having been forgiven what cannot be repaid. The community that has genuinely received this grace — that has allowed the experience of being forgiven an unpayable debt to form its actual orientation rather than merely informing its theological convictions — is the community that is capable of the forgiveness that Matthew commends. The cultivation of forgiveness in community is therefore not primarily a project of moral development but a project of grace reception — of allowing the grace that the community has received to genuinely form it through the practices of prayer, community worship, regular return to the story of Jesus' death and resurrection, and the honest examination of the interior life that the Sermon on the Mount commends. The capacity to forgive grows in proportion to the depth of one's reception of the grace that grounds it.

Lesson Five: The Presence of Christ Is the Foundation of Mission

Matthew's Gospel ends not with a command alone but with a promise: I am with you always, to the very end of the age. This promise is not an addendum to the commission. It is its foundation. The disciples are sent to make disciples of all nations — a task whose scope exceeds anything that human capacity and determination can accomplish — and the basis on which they are sent is not their own competence but the abiding presence of the one who sends them.

This lesson has direct and practical implications for how communities of faith approach their responsibilities. The tendency to measure faithfulness by visible results, to treat mission as a project to be managed toward success, and to locate the energy of the community in its own enthusiasm and organization — all of these tendencies are addressed by Matthew's final word. The foundation is not human effort but divine presence. The Great Commission is not a burden to be discharged but an invitation to participate in what the risen Christ is already doing in the world.

The promise of the abiding presence of Christ is the fulfillment of the Immanuel announcement with which Matthew's Gospel opens. The child born of Mary will be called Immanuel — God with us. The Gospel that opened with this announcement closes with its confirmation and extension: I am with you always, to the very end of the age. The presence of God with his people that was the fundamental promise of the covenant from its beginning has found its definitive and permanent expression in the risen Christ who promises to remain with his community not merely for a period but always, not merely until some future event but to the very end of the age.

This means that the community's engagement with its mission is never a unilateral exercise of its own capacities. It is always a participation in a work that is already underway — the work that the risen Christ is doing in the world through the community he has commissioned. The community does not start the work from a position of absence and try to create what would not otherwise exist. It joins a work that is already in progress, contributing what it has been given in the specific places and circumstances where it has been located, trusting that the one who promised to be always present is actually present and actually working even when the community cannot observe the results of that work.

The mission that Matthew's Great Commission launches has a specific character that shapes how it can legitimately be fulfilled. It is a mission to all nations — genuinely universal in scope, crossing every boundary of ethnicity, culture, language, and social organization. It is a mission of making disciples rather than merely making converts — of forming fully shaped people rather than recruiting adherents. And it is a mission of baptizing and teaching everything Jesus has commanded — not a selected portion chosen for palatability, not a reduced version designed to minimize the demands that the whole makes, but the genuine whole with all its challenges intact. Communities that systematically omit portions of Matthew's teaching from the formation of disciples — whether because those portions are theologically uncomfortable or because they are culturally unpopular — are not fulfilling the commission. They are offering a reduced version of the kingdom in place of the whole.

The community that genuinely rests in the promise of Matthew 28 does not need to measure its faithfulness by visible results, does not need to generate its own enthusiasm as the primary energy of mission, and does not need to manage the impression it makes on those outside it as the primary means of extending the kingdom's reach. It needs only to go, to baptize, to teach, to love the vulnerable it encounters, to practice the forgiveness it has received, to build the community that chapter 18 describes, and to trust the one who has promised to be always present, that the rest will be accomplished by means that exceed its own capacities and its own visibility.

Matthew's Gospel will keep giving back more as its readers keep bringing more to it. The conversation that Matthew's Jesus initiates in the first century continues into every subsequent century with the same invitation and the same expectation: come and learn, hear and do, follow and be formed. That invitation remains open. These five lessons are one way of accepting it.

Closing Reflection

"And surely I am with you always, to the very end of the age."
— Matthew 28:20

Matthew's Gospel has endured because the questions it carries are not going away. Who is Jesus, and what does his coming mean for how life is to be lived? What does genuine righteousness look like, and what is its source? What kind of community does the kingdom of heaven call into being, and by what practices is that community sustained? These are not questions that belong to the first century alone. They are questions that each generation must face with the seriousness they deserve.

What gives Matthew its lasting power is not merely the quality of the teaching it preserves, though that teaching has shaped the moral imagination of Western civilization more profoundly than almost any other body of literature. It is the claim at its center — that in the person of Jesus of Nazareth, the God of Israel acted decisively to fulfill what had been promised, to establish a new covenant community, and to commission that community for a mission that extends to the ends of the earth. This claim is either true, or it is not, and Matthew does not allow its readers to hold it at a comfortable distance. It presses for a response.

One of the most characteristic features of Matthew's Gospel, observed across the entire history of its reception, is its refusal to release the reader once it has been genuinely encountered. Those who bring to it the honest engagement it deserves consistently find that it presses them further than they intended to go, addresses them at levels they did not anticipate, and makes claims on their lives that are more comprehensive and more demanding than any initial reading could prepare them for. Matthew is designed to be revisited rather than simply read once. Its depth is not all visible on the surface. The reader who has read it ten times begins to notice the connections between its parts, the way the narrative and the discourses illuminate each other, the way later passages reshape the understanding of earlier ones. The reader who has spent a lifetime with Matthew finds that it continues to yield insight that previous readings did not reach and to address conditions that previous encounters did not fully engage.

What Matthew Has Given to the World

The influence of Matthew's Gospel on the history of Western civilization is both undeniable and frequently underestimated, because so much of it is embedded in the assumptions and values of the culture it shaped rather than being attributed to its source. The conviction that every human being possesses inherent dignity not contingent on their social usefulness owes more to Matthew's identification of Christ with the hungry and the sick and the imprisoned than to any philosophical argument about personhood. The conviction that power must be exercised in service of those over whom it is held owes more to Matthew's portrait of Jesus giving his life as a ransom for many than to any political philosophy about legitimate authority. The conviction that forgiveness is both possible and necessary for human community owes more to Matthew's community discourse and the parable of the unforgiving servant than to any psychological theory about letting go of grievance.

This does not mean that Western civilization has been particularly good at embodying Matthew's vision of the kingdom. Institutions founded in the name of Matthew's Jesus have been used to justify conquest, slavery, and the persecution of those who did not share their beliefs. The language of Matthew's Gospel has been invoked in the service of causes that its own teaching would condemn without hesitation. Acknowledging this history is not a reason to abandon Matthew. It is a reason to read it more carefully and more honestly — to insist that the claims of the text be taken seriously enough to challenge the communities that invoke it. The woes of Matthew 23 are not addressed only to the scribes and Pharisees of first-century Judaism. They are addressed, in every generation, to the community that reads them.

The Enduring Questions

The questions that Matthew's Gospel raises cannot be finally answered by any human arrangement and will therefore continue to press themselves on every community and every individual in every era. They are questions about what human beings are for, what genuine flourishing consists of, where authority comes from and how it is rightly exercised, how community is built and sustained across the fractures of human failure.

These questions are currently being asked with unusual urgency in Western culture, because the frameworks that previously provided answers to them — the institutional frameworks of organized religion, the civic frameworks of shared democratic values, the social frameworks of stable community life — have eroded significantly, leaving many people without an adequate context for either asking or answering the questions that Matthew addresses. Matthew's response to this condition is the same response it has always offered: here is the one who is the kingdom's announcement and embodiment; come and see, come and learn, come and be formed.

The Character of Sustained Reading

Reading Matthew well over a lifetime requires the cultivation of specific habits of reading that do not develop without intention and practice. The most important is the habit of bringing one's actual experience to the text rather than leaving it at the door. Matthew is not designed to be read as a theological document whose significance is independent of the specific circumstances of

the reader's life. It is designed to address those circumstances —
to engage the actual questions, actual failures, actual relationships,
actual fears, and actual hopes that constitute the reader's
experience.

The reader who brings their experience of betrayal to
Matthew's account of Judas will find something that the reader
who reads it only as historical narrative cannot access. The reader
who brings their experience of failure of nerve to Peter's denial
will find something that the reader who reads it only as biography
cannot find. The text meets the reader where they actually are, and
the depth of the meeting is proportional to the honesty with
which the reader brings their actual situation to the encounter.

The reader who engages Matthew over years and decades will
find that sustained engagement produces a specific kind of
wisdom that cannot be achieved in any other way — not the
wisdom of comprehensive theoretical understanding, but the
wisdom of accumulated encounter. The disciples in Matthew are
not scholars or religious professionals before they are called. They
are fishermen and tax collectors who have been summoned to
something that exceeds their previous experience and who are
formed into it gradually through sustained presence with the one
who calls them. Matthew's formation of its readers follows the
same pattern: it does not require extraordinary preparation or
exceptional capacity. It requires the willingness to keep showing
up, to keep bringing one's actual experience, and to keep allowing
the text to do the work it is designed to do.

The Permanent Invitation

The invitation that Matthew extends — come, follow me — is the
same invitation it extends to every reader who encounters it in
every subsequent generation. It is addressed to people who do not
fully understand what they are agreeing to, who will fail in ways
they do not anticipate, who will need to be restored more times

than they expect, and who will discover gradually and imperfectly the dimensions of what they have accepted that their initial response could not have prepared them for.

Matthew was not written to produce people who have understood the Gospel completely and are living it out with consistent adequacy. It was written to produce people who are in the process of being formed — who have accepted the invitation, who are engaged in the formation it calls for, and who are discovering along the way that the one who called them is adequate to every dimension of the life that following him requires.

For readers who bring to Matthew the honest and sustained engagement it deserves, the most important thing the Gospel contains is not the theological sophistication of its argument, not the literary achievement of its narrative, not the historical significance of its claims, but the specific, personal, concrete promise of the risen Christ: I am with you always, to the very end of the age. Everything else in the Gospel is preparation for, elaboration of, and demonstration of this promise. Everything the community of faith is called to be and do in the world flows from it.

Matthew's Gospel ends where genuine faith always finds its rest — not in its own resources, not in the achievements of the community, not in the sophistication of its theology, but in the promise of the one who calls and sends and remains. That promise has not been broken. It will not be. And the conversation that Matthew's Jesus initiates in the first century continues into every subsequent century, inviting every generation to accept the same invitation that the disciples accepted on the shores of Galilee — and discovering in that acceptance the same presence, the same formation, and the same mission that Matthew has always described as the character of life in the kingdom that has come near.

The Bible for Modern Life Series

This book is part of **The Bible for Modern Life** series—an ongoing collection that explores the meaning, historical setting, and message of individual books of Scripture.

Each volume looks closely at the biblical text to help readers understand what it meant in its original context and how its truths still apply to life today.

The goal is simple: to help modern readers engage more deeply with the Bible—one book at a time.

— Samuel Whitaker

www.ingramcontent.com/pod-product-compliance
Lightning Source LLC
Chambersburg PA
CBHW021329060726
47591CB00006B/1939